SAM SHEPARD

CASEBOOKS ON
MODERN DRAMATISTS
(VOL. 2)

GARLAND REFERENCE LIBRARY
OF THE HUMANITIES
(VOL. 861)

CASEBOOKS ON MODERN DRAMATISTS
(*General Editor:* Kimball King)

SAM SHEPARD
A Casebook

Kimball King

GARLAND PUBLISHING, INC. • NEW YORK & LONDON
1988

Library of Congress Cataloging-in-Publication Data

Sam Shepard : a casebook.

(Garland reference library of the humanities ;
vol. 861. Casebooks on modern dramatists ; vol. 2)
Bibliography: p.
1. Shepard, Sam, 1943– —Criticism and interpretation. I. King, Kimball. II. Series: Garland
reference library of the humanities ; vol. 861.
III. Series: Garland reference library of the
humanities. Casebooks on modern
dramatists ; vol. 2.
PS3569.H394Z87 1988 812'.54 88-24313
ISBN 0–8240–4448–7 (alk. paper)

Printed on acid-free, 250-year-life paper
Manufactured in the United States of America

CONTENTS

GENERAL EDITOR'S NOTE

Sam Shepard: A Casebook is the second in a series of collected essays on recent British and American playwrights published by Garland Publishing, Inc. It follows *Tom Stoppard: A Casebook* and precedes forthcoming casebooks on Caryl Churchill and Christopher Hampton. The Shepard collection includes articles, requested specifically for this volume, of scholars identified with major critical appraisals of the author's work. Because Shepard is one of the world's most prolific writers for the stage, I have selected articles that suggest his range and complexity and that often focus on his better known achievements, such as his Pulitzer Prize-winning *Buried Child*. There are, however, perceptive discussions of Shepard's less famous works which contribute to an understanding of his impact on twentieth century drama. Included are a variety of critical approaches, bibliographical, biographical, historical, new critical and post-structuralist, all of which attempt to elucidate the wide-ranging appeal and power of Sam Shepard's plays.

Kimball King
General Editor

INTRODUCTION

Having written more than thirty plays in a decade and a half, Sam Shepard is one of this country's most inventive and prolific playwrights. Television, old movies, and romantic American myths provide him with characters and settings. He has a fine ear for the sixties' vernacular, especially apparent in the conversations of characters who belong to the drug or rock music cultures, and his outrageously funny protagonists deliver monologues of absurd but entertaining complexity. Frequently the playwright hints that he is nostalgic for an age when simple heroes could be praised for honest values. Anachronisms of time and setting, such as his linking of Mae West and Marlene Dietrich with Paul Bunyan and Jesse James in *Mad Dog Blues*, allow him to mix fantasy and folklore with social commentary. Other plays combine pop music and biography to produce a media event like *Seduced*, which presents the haunting story of a man who resembles Howard Hughes. Critics of Shepard sometimes lament his loose plot construction, his occasionally improbable dialogue, and his extravagant use of symbols or dream elements, but they cannot overlook his wild new talent which is both comical and disturbing. Winner of an Obie Award for "sustained achievement" in the theatre, he also received in 1979 a Pulitzer Prize for *Buried Child*.

This casebook presents original essays on a range of subjects covering the playwright's impressive career. From his earliest works to his most recent plays Shepard is regarded as a source of energy in the American theatre. Since John Osborne's *Look Back In Anger* opened at the Royal Court Theatre on May 8, 1956, British dramatists have dominated the theatre world. Of course, American theatre has been distinguished by Albee's contributions, as well by Kopit's, Lanford Wilson's, David Mamet's and others'. Nevertheless Shepard has increasingly become the focus of critical contention throughout the world, evidenced by the fact that our contributors live as far apart as New Zealand and Ontario. Shepard is a media personality as well as a playwright; his success as a film star, his handsome appearance and his highly publicized relationship with cinema star, Jessica Lange, have doubtless contributed to his fame. As editor of this volume, I have been anxious to reveal a wide range of critical opinions toward Shepard's work—from close readings of individual works to post-structuralist interpretations of their impact on audiences.

Above all I have tried to preserve the sense of fun, even exhilaration, which accompanies an effective production of a Shepard play. Serious scholarship need not be pedantic nor humorless. The essayists were attracted to their choice of topics because they have zestful personalities of their own as well as intellectual curiosity about the Shepard "phenomenon." To refresh the memories of readers about biographical factors and the sequence of performances a chronology is offered in the front of the casebook and at its conclusion there is an annotated bibliography which might form the basis of additional readings on the subject.

Essays have been arranged mostly on the basis of their chronological order. Therefore, it is appropriate to begin with Patrick Fennell's investigation of the young artist.

Fennell wrote an article on *Angel City* for the *Educational Theatre Journal* in 1977; in the same year he completed his dissertation, *Sam Shepard: The Flesh and Blood of Theatre*. Fennell is especially interested in those of Shepard's plays which were produced and not published and those which were neither produced nor published. He refers to them wittily as "Shepard's Lost Sheep" and offers them as witnesses to Shepard's earliest creative preoccupation with certain themes and myths which pervade his entire career. The playwright's dazzling experimentation is described admiringly but critically. Works such as *Blue Bitch*, *Dog*, *In a Coma*, *Jacaranda*, *Jackson's Dance*, *Man Fly*, *Red Woman*, *The Rocking Chair*, and *Up to Thursday* are regarded not only as preparations for Shepard's acclaimed later works but also as imaginative exercises in ideas and actions for a revitalized American theatre.

Albert Wilhelm has concentrated on a lesser-known Shepard play that has attracted the attention of several authors in this collection including Auerbach, who alludes to it in the title of her essay. Wilhelm delves into the Icarus-Daedalus myth in great detail, never claiming that Shepard is "a careful student of classical myth." Instead he argues that "whether or not he [Shepard] actually knows the small details of the Daedalus story, his life and plays happen to be full of diverse embodiments of mythic materials." Convincingly, Wilhelm shows that the process of transformation itself, whether it be the author's attempt to enhance his personal history with exaggerations or the attempts of his characters to create their own roles in life, is the crucial subject matter of Shepard's plays. By studying the father-son, mother-son roles in *Icarus's Mother* as well as the motif of the rebellious son and of the explorer, perhaps narcissist, who wishes to soar above others, Wilhelm provides an interpretative key to much of the Shepard canon.

Elizabeth Proctor wrote her dissertation on *The Art of Sam Shepard*. Her present essay concentrates on two of the most widely discussed aspects of Shepard's talent: his special brand of comedy and the "mythic" implications of his subject matter. Both are intrinsically American because they are rooted in the sort of paradoxes which bedeviled our Puritan ancestors—how can men, who are all sinners, discover a new Eden? Their efforts are inevitably futile not only because they are naively Utopian but also because they are the products of competing or incompatible desires. Proctor therefore explores incongruity as a major source of humor in Shepard's plays, concentrating on the seeming absurdities of dialogue and situation in seldom discussed works, such as *La Turista* and *The Unseen Hand*. She also reveals that the incongruities which create comic theatrical situations demand myths which have traditionally contained the power to reconcile opposing forces. Significantly she parts company with critics who attach portentous, neo-Jungian intent to Shepard's use of American history and popular culture. Instead, she emphasizes the non-intellectual aspects of Shepard's myths which she prefers to see as "mysteries," a distinction which the playwright has himself insisted upon: "By myth I mean a sense of mystery and not necessarily a traditional formula." The comedy and the mystery which Shepard dramatizes reflect the innate chaos of man's nature and society. Only through his own imaginative efforts as an artist—a role Shepard accepts with reservations and self-depreciation—can he create the illusion of order, an illusion which can be sustained only in a theatrical context.

Proctor's detailed reading of the *Mad Dog Blues* and *Forensic and the Navigators* expose the ways in which Shepard's myths are like mysteries. Her juxtaposition in one essay of four critically neglected plays permits us to see the relationship of incongruity and disorder to both the comic and "mythic" (or mysterious) elements that have brought Shepard fame.

In 1982 Doris Auerbach wrote a book length study called *Sam Shepard, Arthur Kopit and Off Broadway*. Her article for this collection returns to a motif she exposed in her earlier work, the presence of "dominated, powerless mother figures." Shepard's *Lie of the Mind*, written after Auerbach had published her book, provides additional examples of "mothers too weak to counteract the violence of the father."

Auerbach adds, "They lack the will and power to restore order in their world, to bring about a family in balance, one that can nurture its children." Several essayists in this volume are distressed by Shepard's vision of an American society which appears unable to provide a stable, nurturing environment for new generations. Beginning with *Buried Child* and continuing through *True West, Fool for Love* and *Lie of the Mind*, Auerbach traces both the patterns of family violence and Shepard's portrayal of the women who might oppose it. Interestingly, she relates the malaise of domestic life to its seeming antithesis, the solitary existence of the frontiersman or desert recluse. Shepard's "West" is a world primarily characterized by a lack of human commitment—an escape from civilizing influences more than an edenic wilderness with the potential for innocence. In selecting the title for her present essay, Auerbach alludes not only to the title of a Shepard play but also to a mythical archetype of a forgotten and ineffectual woman, when she asks: "Who was Icarus's Mother?"

"Story Itself: *Curse of the Starving Class* through *Fool for Love*" was written by Christopher Brookhouse, an English professor at the University of North Carolina who recently took early retirement to devote more time to writing fiction. His most critically acclaimed novels are *Running Out* (1970) and *Wintermute* (1978), and he has published a volume of poetry, *Scattered Light* (1969), as well as numerous scholarly treatises, both in the area of film criticism and medieval studies. Not unexpectedly he focuses on a topic of interest to any writer: "Story Itself." Shepard's characters are storytellers and his plays are renowned for their lengthy monologues. Brookhouse believes that a self-consciousness about the storytelling process, revealed in dialogue, causes Shepard's audiences "to become aware of the relationship and truth or invention of the content of the story that is being told." Characters appear to create fantasies both about the past and about the future. Consequently, the truth of any person or group is never substantiated although the storytelling mode invites the audience to speculate, to form opinions about the dynamics of a particular personality or family—perhaps about the author himself. There are curious connections among the four plays Brookhouse has chosen to discuss. *Curse of the Starving Class* and *Buried Child* are experiments in storytelling and in teasing audiences to compare their assumptions with the author's version of events. *True West* and *Fool for Love* are more flagrantly concerned with the process of storytelling, especially the later play. Yet Brookhouse believes that the structure of *Curse of the Starving Class* parallels that of *True West* while that of *Buried Child* more closely anticipates *Fool for Love*. All of Shepard's "stories," he discovers, are Shepard's conversations with his audiences and challenges to their own creative powers of storytelling; inevitably, we, as observers, become linked both to the characters and the author.

Jane Ann Crum was dramaturg for the Center Stage Theatre in Baltimore for the production of *Buried Child,* which opened in April 1986. She brings a unique perspective for this volume in that she has been responsible for creating a stage atmosphere which could depict the intentions of the playwright's text. As Crum points out, she was always aware of her "social accountability" as an interpreter of Shepard's play. She notes that interpretation "becomes an act of selection" but adds that the selection process "hinges on the mysterious communion between the text, the artist, and the audience." It is intriguing to see how costume, set design and actors' movements are intended to reflect Shepard's ideas. Crum believes that what *Buried Child* offers is "the possibility of change." She outlines the origins of her commitment to the production of the play and the process of its implementation.

"Character Behavior and the Fantastic in Buried Child" is the work of Bruce Mann of Oakland University, who wrote his master's thesis on O'Neill's *Long Day's Journey Into Night* and his doctoral dissertation on Tennessee Williams. While both of these dramatists were noted for the psychological credibility of their characters and lent themselves to Freudian criticism or stood the test of Stanislavski's recognizable "motivation," Shepard has created a new sort of dramatic character, one not derived from the literary mode of his predecessors in the theatre, but rather from what Mann calls "the fantastic mode." Stage movement and the actors' behavior in a Shepard play cannot be systematically evaluated by the methods we would use when scrutinizing an Arthur Miller drama. By Miller's standards Shepard's characters would be considered shallow, weird or possibly schizophrenic. But Shepard has a far different vision of life than the author of "Tragedy and the Common Man."

Mann defines the fantastic mode after the principles of A.B. Chanady who claimed that such a mode incorporated two levels of reality: the everyday world based on conventions and reasonable behaviour and a supernatural one which defies logic and exudes mystery. For Shepard the overlapping of these two worlds—the worlds of realism and absurdity, perhaps, demands a script which can exploit the incongruities and mysteries of life. The characters in his plays, according to Mann "present themselves to Shepard's imagination as Personalities with Identity-projects." And at the core of each play are "regenerative myths that defy everyday logic but that surface constantly" to influence the characters and to create an often unnerving triumph of fantasy over reality.

Ron Mottram wrote the first book-length study of Shepard devoted entirely to that author's work: *Inner Landscapes: The Theatre of Sam Shepard* (1984). Here he continues his evaluation of Shepard's major themes and techniques in "Exhaustion of the American Soul: Sam Shepard's *A Lie of the Mind*." Although the material Shepard draws upon in his most recent play is familiar, Mottram believes the play's major strength is its "structural integrity." The male characters in *Lie of the Mind* characteristically "cause pain and rend the fabric of family life." Nevertheless, Mottram believes *Lie* may depart from Shepard's earlier plays in a significant area; for the first time in the author's work Mottram finds a suggestion that "ingrained male hate and violence might be healed." Mottram also asserts that Beth is the central character of the play, parting company with critics who lament her ineffectuality. In order to clarify his assertions about Shepard's mastery of structure, Mottram devotes a segment of his essay to an inventory, in the form of a chart, which specifies interconnections between actors, stage directions and language, proving that the characters remain linked with each other "even while they remain separated in their own spaces."

In the December 1987 issue of *Modern Drama* Leonard Wilcox published an article entitled "Modernism Vs. Postmodernism: Shepard's

Tooth of the Crime and the Discourses of Popular Culture." For this volume Wilcox has written an essay which clarifies many enigmas of *Red Cross* (1968). Taking a post-structuralist approach and drawing on inspiration both from Freudian and Lacanian analytic theory and Julia Kristeva's feminist exploration of the problems of signification, Wilcox reveals that Shepard's plays have both a manifest and literal content, comparable in some regards to a Freudian dream, and, also, that they expose conflicts between "maternal authority" and "paternal law" (Kristeva's terms) which undergird the power struggle between Jim and his nurse in Shepard's startling play. In *Powers of Horror* Kristeva described the "abjection" of women in a patriarchal society and the necessity of a "fully constructed subject" to enter into the symbolic (male-dominated) order by rejecting/dominating the female. The female must either pay obeisance to phallic dominance, identifying with power, or shun power altogether, fleeing from the phallic and denying her right to enter history. The otherwise inexplicable role changes between Jim and his nurse in *Red Cross* and Jim's seemingly ridiculous need to divert his nurse from her task of changing his bed linen by giving her swimming lessons (on the bed) makes sense in the context of a world where maternal nurturing struggles continually against paternal censorship and disapproval. Wilcox concludes that the power of *Red Cross* lies partly in Shepard's special attitude toward language. The blood which gushes forth from Jim's forehead at the conclusion of the play is a non-verbal device which, according to Wilcox, suggests like Oedipus' wound, the problematic relation between desire and language at the heart of Shepard's play. Entering the phallic world of language, as Kristeva would say, stimulates desires which paradoxically cannot find fulfillment in language. Wilcox's perceptive study of *Red Cross* reveals that even Shepard's earliest plays, considered merely bizarre or unformed by critics twenty years ago, had the potential to transform contemporary drama.

Phyllis Randall's essay, "Adapting to Reality: Language in Shepard's *Curse of the Starving Class*," demonstrates that the playwright has been able to transfer the innovative verbal games and comic parodies of vernacular speech and the quasi-absurdist devices of his earlier, nearly surrealistic plays to a dramatic format with broader popular appeal—one which emphasizes the "realism" of his work, permitting his emergence from notoriety as an *enfant terrible* of nineteen-sixties theatre into widely respected authorship in the nineteen-seventies and eighties. Randall summarizes the accolades Shepard has received for his creative use of language but reveals the lack of critical material attempting to account for the mixed success of his characters' frequently bizarre monologues and dialogues.

Asserting that *Curse of the Starving Class, Buried Child, True West* are critically considered his "best" plays—those which Shepard himself describes as a "family trilogy"—Randall concentrates on Shepard's linguistic devices in *Curse of the Starving Class* to illustrate the playwright's evolution from a fledgling writer whose stage language mirrored the vernacular speech, consumer art and counter-culture music (both rock, and country and western) of the post-modernist period, to the master whose words reveal psychological realities and societal truths.

From the beginning of his career Shepard's characters have often been described as inventing several voices in order, as Randall notes, "to discover which one is mine." In "vintage" Shepard plays, if we can refer to the works of a forty-year-old artist in such terms, the playwright creates powerful language for his actors to speak by emphasizing the reality of the thought processes of his characters, rather than by observing traditional rules of stage conversation and etiquette. Facades are stripped away and we are given a more intimate glimpse of motivation.

In *Curse of the Starving Class* Shepard manages to find more natural reasons for his characters to speak in different voices than he found in earlier plays. For example, Randall points out that Weston's obscene drunken speech is "converted" when he undergoes an "epiphany" upon discovering a filled refrigerator. Emma's several voices correspond to the biological and emotional mood swings of her adolescent state, so that her conversation is at times either childish or mature or both. Ella is established as a liar with distinctly ambivalent feelings toward her family. Therefore we can expect her words to be alternately nurturing and sympathetic, or evasive and calculating. Finally, Randall concludes that Wesley's speech patterns, from artist-seer to hypocrite-poseur, correspond to his transformation from idealist into a carbon copy of his worthless father, precluding an optimistic interpretation of the play's outcome. Of particular interest in Randall's essay are her allusions to Brechtian and Pinteresque devices in Shepard's speech which are sometimes effective, sometimes not; her particular use of the term "solo" to describe a version of monologue iconoclastically

Shepard's; and the suggestion of a non-verbal "lyricism" that on-stage events, such as frying bacon, can evoke.

Anne Wilson, a professor at the University of Guelph in Ontario, wrote her dissertation on Sam Shepard and is also contributing to the Garland casebook on Christopher Hampton. Unabashedly she refers to Shepard as "the pre-eminent playwright of the contemporary theatre." Her article in this volume is entitled Great Expectations: Language and the Problem of Presence in Sam Shepard's Writing." Her post-structuralist interpretation of his works is related to Jane Ann Crum's concept of dramaturg, Christopher Brookhouse's investigation of storytelling and Phyllis Randall's study of language. Wilson places Shepard in the tradition of Emerson and Walt Whitman in that while he is not a transcendentalist, he shares the transcendentalist's yearning for a merger of the signifier and the signification in almost spiritual terms. Wilson notes that Shepard once compared a mystical experience at a musical "jamming" session as being similar to a visitation by the Holy Ghost. She does not claim that Shepard's theatre is evangelical "but rather that his sense of language gives it a theological impulse." She adds that Shepard "seeks to discover within himself the language which will make the significance fully present." In this sense Shepard is comparable to Walt Whitman whose wish to share his mystical experiences constituted a poetic impulse that inspired his finest work. But the poetic impulse is as grandly doomed to end in public disbelief as Cassandra's prophecies. Still Wilson places Shepard in the romantic tradition as he searches for the spiritual world behind the material. It is fitting that Shepard's many allusions to the frontier should represent to Wilson the gap between "language" and "presence" since, after all, the frontier is a "borderline" between civilization and wilderness which must necessarily exist always in the future (or cease to be a frontier). Paradoxically, only through a fictional representation of the West or any other setting is the "true self" of Shepard or his character realized.

Tommy Thompson is a musician and a member of the Red Clay Ramblers who provided the musical backdrop for Shepard's *Lie of the Mind* and his forthcoming movie, *Far North*. Shepard first learned of the Ramblers from a poster of *Diamond Studs: The Life of Jesse James* (book by Jim Wann; music and lyrics by Bland Simpson and Jim Wann). Thompson, Simpson and Wann have close ties to Chapel Hill and the University of North Carolina, and I have enjoyed knowing them all for many years. Thompson has written about his professional relationship with the playwright and their friendship. He notes that Shepard is "a musician, himself" and, as a result, knows "how a roughed-in piece will work when it's been refined and placed." He provides insights into the relationship of music to dialogue in Shepard's plays, especially when he says that Shepard often urged the use of a "song or melody that, instead of supporting an actor's lines, would undercut it with irony." Thompson's essay adds a highly personal and appropriate conclusion to this collection of essays honoring an outstanding playwright.

CHRONOLOGY

1943	Sam Shepard is born Sam Shepard Rogers, Jr. on November 5, in Fort Sheridan, Illinois, to Samuel Shepard and Elaine Schook Rogers.
1943–55	Shepard's family lives on army bases in South Dakota, Utah, Florida, and Guam.
1955	The family settles in California, first in South Pasadena, and then on an avocado ranch in Duarte. Shepard works with ranch animals, and one year has the grand champion yearling ram at the Los Angeles County Fair. For a while, he wants to be a vet. He also begins playing the drums, his first involvement with rock and roll.
1961	Shepard graduates from Duarte, a California high school. He enrolls in Mount Antonio Junior College, but stays only one year.
1962	Shepard joins the Bishop's Company, travelling with it until it arrives in New York. Shepard says, "I realized suddenly that anybody can make theatre."
1963	Shepard remains in New York when the troupe leaves, and officially changes his name. He works as a waiter at the Village Gate, a jazz club. He plays "cowboys" in the streets with his friend Charles Mingus, Jr.

1964   *Cowboys* and *Rock Garden* are performed at Theatre Genesis at St. Mark's Church in-the-Bowery. A favorable review by Michael Smith in *The Village Voice* encourages Shepard to continue writing.

1965   Six Shepard plays are performed: *Up to Thursday* (which Shepard calls "a bad exercise in absurdity"), at Theatre 65; *Dog* and *Rocking Chair*, at La Mama Experimental Theatre Club; *Chicago* (which Shepard says he wrote in one day), at Theatre Genesis; *Icarus's Mother*, at Cafe Cino; and *4H Club*, at Theatre 65. Shepard is still working as a waiter, at Marie's Crisis Cafe.

1966   *Fourteen Hundred Thousand* debuts at Firehouse Theatre in Minneapolis. *Red Cross* is performed at Judson's Poet's Theatre. Shepard is the first playwright to receive three Obies in one year, winning for *Chicago*, *Icarus's Mother*, and *Red Cross*.

1967   Four Shepard plays are produced: *La Turista* (which Shepard says is "the first play I ever rewrote"), at American Place Theatre; *Melodrama Play*, at La Mama Experimental Theatre Club; *Cowboys No. 2*, at Mark Taper Forum in Los Angeles; and *Forensic and the Navigators* (which was followed by a rock concert, with Shepard on drums), at Theatre Genesis. *La Turista* wins an Obie Award.

              Shepard's movie career begins, with his first screenplay, *Me and My Brother*. He also works with the Italian director Michelangelo Antonioni on the movie *Zabriskie Point*, which is released in 1969. Fellowships from the University of Minnesota and Yale, as well as a Rockefeller Grant, end Shepard's work as a waiter.

1968   Shepard is awarded a Guggenheim Fellowship, as well as Obies for *Forensic and the Navigators* and *Melodrama Play*. He played drums and guitar with the Holy Modal Bounders.

1969   Shepard marries O-Lan Johnson at St. Mark's Church-in-the-Bowery. *The Holy Ghostly* is produced by La Mama Touring Co., and *The Unseen Hand* is produced by La Mama Experimental Theatre Club. *Fourteen Hundred Thousand* appears on National Educational Television. Excerpts from *Rock Garden* appear in *Oh Calcutta!* at the Eden Theatre in New York.

1970   A son, Jesse Mojo, is born. *Operation Sidewinder*, Shepard's most lavish production to date, appears at the Repertory Company of Lincoln Center, and *Shaved Splits* is produced by La Mama Experimental Theatre Club. He acts in the movie *Brand X*.

1971   Shepard and his family move to London. Back in New York, Shepard's work returns to off-Off-Broadway. *Mad Dog Blues* is produced by Theatre Genesis. *Cowboy Mouth*, written with Patti Smith, appears in Edinburgh at Traverse Theatre, and in New York at American Place Theatre. *Back Bog Beast Bait* appears at American Place Theatre. *Nightwalk* and *Terminal* are written with Megan Terry and Jean-Claude van Itallie. Shepard also writes the screenplay *Ringaleevio* with Murray Mednick.

1972   *The Tooth of Crime* is produced in Britain at Open Space Theatre and in the United States at Princeton University. Four other Shepard plays are produced in London.

1973   *Blue Bitch* appears on BBC Television. *The Tooth of Crime* is awarded an Obie. *Hawkmoon*, a collection of poetry and prose, is published.

1974   *Geography of a Horse Dreamer* and *Action* are produced at Theatre Upstairs, in London. This is the first play Shepard directs. *Little Ocean* is produced at the prestigious Hampstead Theatre Club, in London. Shepard and his family return to California.

1975   *Action* opens simultaneously at Magic Theatre in San Fransisco and American Place Theatre in New York and is awarded an Obie. *Killer's Head* also appears at American Place Theatre. The Magic Theatre becomes Shepard's primary theatre.

1976   *Angel City* appears at Magic Theatre, *Suicide in B Flat* appears at Yale Repertory Theatre. Shepard is also awarded a Brandeis Creative Arts Medal. He writes a one act opera, *The Sad Lament of Pecos Bill on the Eve of Killing his Wife*.

1977   *Inacoma* is produced, with the help of a $15,000 Rockefeller Grant, at Magic Theatre. *Curse of the Starving Class* is awarded an Obie as the best new American play. *The Rolling Thunder Logbook*, a travel journal of a tour made with Bob Dylan and Allen Ginsberg, is published.

1978   *Buried Child* opens at Magic Theatre and at Yale Repertory Theatre, and then has a run of one hundred and fifty-two performances at New York's Theatre de Lys. Shepard acts in the movie *Days of Heaven*.

1979   Shepard is awarded a Pulitzer Prize (as well as an Obie) for *Buried Child*, which is one of the few plays never produced on Broadway to win a Pulitzer. *Tongues* and *Savage/Love*, written with Joseph Chaikin, are produced at Magic Theatre and at the NY Shakespeare Festival. *Seduced* is produced at American Place Theatre. Shepard writes the libretto *Jacaranda*, which is produced at St. Clement's Church in New York.

1980   *True West* opens at the Magic Theatre, and eventually
            runs for seven hundred and sixty-two performances in
            New York's Cherry Lane Theatre. Shepard appears
            with Ellen Burstyn in the film *Resurrection*.

1981   Shepard acts in the film *Raggedy Man*.

1982   *Motel Chronicles*, a collection of poetry and prose, is
            published. Shepard acts in *Frances*, with Jessica
            Lange.

1983   La Mama Experimental Theatre Company puts on
            Superstitions, a group of sketches from *Motel
            Chronicles*. *Fool for Love* opens at the Magic
            Theatre, and then in New York. It wins the Obie for
            best new American play of the year. Shepard appears
            in *The Right Stuff*.

1984   Shepard writes the screenplay *Paris, Texas*, which
            wins the Palme d'Or at Cannes. He appears with
            Jessica Lange in *Country*.

1985   *A Lie of the Mind* opens at the Promenade Theatre in
            New York, and is named the outstanding new play of
            the New York theatre season. A film version of *Fool
            for Love*, as well as a radio version of *The War in
            Heaven*, written with Joseph Chaikin, are produced.

1986   A daughter, Hannah, is born to Shepard and Jessica
            Lange. Shepard and Lange appear in the film *Crimes
            of the Heart*.

1987   A second child, Samuel, is born to Shepard and
            Lange. *True Dylan*, a one-act play, is published in
            Esquire.

Sam Shepard

SHEPARD'S LOST SHEEP

Patrick J. Fennell

Sam Shepard is one of the most prolific playwrights in the history of American drama. Aside from his canon of over thirty published plays and monologues, several of his plays have been produced but never published. Still others were never published nor produced. Moreover, countless others remain unfinished. These plays might be located in university libraries, in Shepard's possession, at the theatres where they were produced, or, as is often the case, collected by the curious dramaturgical detective in search of the "lost" plays of Sam Shepard.

This article will be a sampling of the content and style of some of Shepard's unpublished works from 1964 to 1979, offering an overview of the development of a playwright.

Shepard's earliest recollection of writing provides an interesting perspective of his penchant for writing something highly imaginative:

> I remember when I was a kid, I wrote a story about a coke bottle. Coke bottles had the name of the city where they were manufactured inscribed on the bottom—St. Paul, Dubuque, wherever. So I wrote the story about this bottle and its travels. It would get filled up in one town, someone would drink it and throw it out the window, then it would get on a truck and go somewhere else (Cott 170).

Although Shepard's story of the coke bottle might reflect a juvenile affection for the transient powers of objects, it is also most probably his first lost work.

One of Shepard's most significant lost plays is his first play, *Cowboys*. *Cowboys* and another Shepard play, *The Rock Garden*, about the absurdity of being an adolescent in the sixties, opened at Theatre Genesis on October 16, 1964. *Cowboys* was originally written "because Charles [Mingus, Jr.] and me use to run around the streets playing cowboys in New York" (Chubb 4). These are two friends "playing" to create imaginative old cowboy transformations against a New York skyline under construction. Shepard claims: "I wrote the original *Cowboys*, and then I rewrote it and called it 'No. 2', that's all. The original is lost now" (Chubb 4).

Despite Shepard's explanation that *Cowboys #2* is merely a rewrite of *Cowboys*, there is evidence to support the fact that there were elements in *Cowboys* that did not end up in *Cowboys #2*. In an otherwise thoroughly negative and prejudiced review of the play, Jerry Tallmer states that the two men in *Cowboys* "have a falling out over an imaginary canteen, they dive away from police sirens. They practice baseball" (33). None of these events occurs in *Cowboys #2*. Despite Shepard's claim that *Cowboys #2* is merely a rewrite of the original play, the later play was written at a time when Shepard's playwriting talent had grown significantly.

Numerous attempts were made to retrieve the script. None of the individuals involved in the production (Ralph Cooke, director, cast: Robert Lyons, Kevin O'Connor) had copies; nor did Theatre Genesis, the theatre where it was first produced. To this day, it remains one of Shepard's lost plays.

Edward Albee was to remark in 1965 that Shepard gives one the impression "of inventing drama as a form each time he writes a play" (15). Shepard astutely argues this point: "The so called originality of the early work just came from ignorance. I just didn't know" (Chubb 5). Experiments which support Shepard's belief are three unpublished plays during Shepard's early period which evince a post-absurdist vision, albeit with Shepard's own uniquely American adolescent point of view. Like the plays which preceded them, *Up to Thursday*, *Dog* and *The Rocking Chair* are concerned, in a highly theatrical and powerfully imagistic manner, with the absurdity of growing up in America. These plays contain simplistic ideas or images connected with a highly contemporary acting style. Shepard states he "would have [sic] like a picture, and just start from there. A picture of a guy in a bathtub or of two guys on stage and a sign blinking on . . . " (Chubb 6).

Up to Thursday opened on November 23, 1964, at the Village South Theatre. *Up to Thursday* concerns a young man (to be seen again in several other Shepard plays, such as *Operation Sidewinder*), who is pictured in the following stage direction at the opening of the play:

> *A bare stage. Upstage center is a young man seated in a chair. Downstage left is a large rock. As the lights come up the young man sits with his arms hanging at his sides and breathing very deeply. (Up to Thursday 1)*

Construction workers then enter and order the removal of the rock with a crane. The young man protests the rock's removal, an obvious youthful reaction against the destruction of the natural environment. Nevertheless, the large crane removes the rock by the end of the scene. Shepard follows this rather desultory scene with an interesting theatrical image, to key in scene II:

> *The Beatles' record, "I Saw Her Standing There," comes on very loudly and plays through the blackout. During the blackout chairs are dropped behind the curtain followed by applause. Four of the characters punch the curtains in time to the music (Up to Thursday 2)*

Scene II opens with the young man lying down on a bed upstage center under an American flag—a powerful simultaneous dual image suggesting adolescent sexuality and at the same time evoking the body of a deceased young veteran shipped home from a war. Two women, Terry and Sherry, and two men, Larry and Harry, are seated Right and Left stage. What follows are an absurd series of boy-girl adolescent games concerning communication, sexuality and alienation. One such game involves a discussion Terry has with Harry concerning her training to run track:

> TERRY: It took a lot of training you know? They say girls have smaller lungs than boys so it takes more conditioning.

HARRY: Terry!
TERRY: I guess that's because girls have titties and boys don't.
        I mean there's more room for lungs in a boy than a
        girl.
HARRY: Terry!
TERRY: I didn't like it that much anyway. It was sorta fun but I
        didn't really like it.
HARRY: Terry!
(*TERRY gets up slowly and crosses over to HARRY, she stands
in front of him. HARRY rises slowly, they kiss passionately
then TERRY crosses back to her seat and sits as before, HARRY
sits, LARRY applauds then stops. (Up to Thursday 2)*

In the final moments of the play, Terry and Harry are under the
flag, and as the same Beatles' song plays, "the movement under the flag
becomes more violent" (*Up to Thursday* 2).

The critics generally agreed with Shepard that *Up to Thursday* "was
a bad exercise in absurdity . . . it was a terrible play, really" (Chubb 8).
Although *Up to Thursday* did not receive acclaim, Off-Off Broadway
offered an opportunity primarily for the development of the
playwright's dramaturgy. Thus, Shepard's next two plays, *Dog* and *The
Rocking Chair*, opened February 10, 1965, at La Mama.

Shepard states that *Dog* "was about a black guy on a park bench, a
sort of *Zoo Story*-type play" (Chubb 8). Indeed, the play is a ten page
confrontation between an old black man and a young man. This
confrontation amounts to be a one-note affair in which a "Negro"
accuses a "Young Man" and everyone else, (as a quasi-absurdist notion
of all people as animals), of being a "dog":

NEGRO: You want to hear the truth?
YOUNG MAN: Yeah.
NEGRO: You're a dog.
YOUNG MAN: A dog?
NEGRO: A dog. (*Dog* 6)

At the end of *Dog*, the Young Man leaves the Negro and in a long
speech demonstrates, for no apparent reason, his inability to sing:

*He opens his mouth extremely wide and strains to give out a
sound but it won't come, he tries again straining for a sound,
the lights dim down. (Dog 10)*

The Rocking Chair concerns still another Young Man who rocks in a rocking chair while a girl reads her short story about a young boy to him. At various intervals the girl goes through everyday tasks such as answering the telephone and the door. As in *The Rock Garden, Up to Thursday* and *Dog*, Shepard experiments with the use of long descriptive monologues in order to evoke mysterious and absurd theatrical experiences based on everyday life. For example, towards the end of the play, a young boy mysteriously enters the young man's room and sits on a bed. (Could this be the young boy who had been the subject of the girl's story earlier?) Eventually, the young man describes his experience of seeing a group of college kids leave a coffee shop. The young man follows their movements away from the coffee shop and back towards him:

> "They got bigger and bigger and looked like they were walking back up the street. I blinked my eyes just for a second because they were getting watery from holding them open so long. And when I opened them they were gone." (*The Rocking Chair* 12)

The theme and style of Shepard's earliest plays would be developed in later one acts such as *4-H Club, Icarus's Mother, Red Cross, Chicago*, and *Fourteen Hundred Thousand*. In a departure from most of the earlier plays, which seem completely aimless and vapid by comparison, at this point Shepard began to develop a comic vision of the world which would appear in many of his later plays. It was also in these plays, in conjunction with the art of the transformation, that Shepard's approach to characterization would begin to reflect an interest in trance and possession states appearing in many of his later plays, beginning with his first full length play, *La Turista* (1967).

Over the next five years, Shepard wrote and produced a variety of plays which dealt with "mythic characters" and developed plots consisting of a "combination science-fiction, Westerns and television" (Shepard *NYT* 49–53), including *Forensic and The Navigators* (1967), *The Holy Ghostly* (1969), *The Unseen Hand* (1969), *Operation Sidewinder* (1970), and *Back Bog Beast Bait* (1971).

In 1972, Shepard moved to England, and wrote five plays over the next two years: *The Tooth of Crime* (1972), *Geography of a Horse Dreamer* (1974), *Action* (1974), and two "lost" unpublished plays, *Blue Bitch* (1973) and *Little Ocean* (1974).

After the success of *The Tooth of Crime* at the Open Space Theatre in London, *Blue Bitch* was shown on BBC Television, and had its American premiere January 18, 1973, at Theatre Genesis in New York. *Blue Bitch* reflected Shepard's newly found interest in dog racing, (a switch from his earlier American interest in horse racing), and the comic trials and tribulations of being an American expatriate couple living in London. The American couple, Cody and Dixie, have put an ad in a British newspaper to sell their "blue bitch" or greyhound dog. A prospective Scottish buyer, whom Cody calls "Donald," calls them to get information. However, all we hear are growls coming from the receiver.

Despite Cody's attempt to understand Donald's growls, he is frustrated in his attempt to communicate with the prospective buyer. This leads Cody to question whether he should sell the dog and return to America. Perhaps, Shepard tries to evoke the geographical displacement he felt at the time. As Cody states at one point in the play: "We *are* in a foreign country you know. Just because they speak the same language doesn't mean a thing" (*Blue Bitch* 18).

Cody's feeling of geographical and psychical displacement eventually leads him to call upon a Cockney Milkman for help. Cody slowly introduces the subject of dog racing until he thinks that the Milkman is in the proper frame of mind. He uses a sort of incantation by describing the British Greyhound racing scene in highly descriptive fragmentary sentences. As Cody's speech builds, the Milkman slowly becomes possessed by some unknown demon. He is panting, hissing and growling, and his face is all contorted. He eventually transforms into a weird canine creature and whimpers around the stage "like a frightened dog" (*Blue Bitch* 24).

Believing that the Milkman won't be able to help them in his possessed state, Cody quits: "At least we found out he can't help us" (*Blue Bitch* 25). A few moments later, the phone rings again. The Milkman answers the phone:

> *The same growling comes from the phone. The MILKMAN listens and growls back. This goes on for awhile. The MILKMAN talking and growling and the phone answering back. When they've finished their conversation, the MILKMAN hangs up and suddenly becomes just like he was before.* (Blue Bitch 29)

Once the Milkman returns to his former state of normalcy, he can explain Donald's offer quite lucidly. Cody is so mystified and perplexed that he states: "That does it. I'm going back to Wyoming." Shortly after the Milkman leaves, the play dissolves without any real resolution. A Postman arrives and sings Cody and Dixie a song to close the play.

Village Voice critic Martin Washburn chides Shepard for using a meandering structure and not resolving the American couple's predicament. He also claims that "we feel for a moment that we may be given a glimpse of Cody (cf. Shepard) himself rather than his style" (Washburn 22). It is apparent, however, that Shepard wrote *Blue Bitch* as an experiment to prepare for his next play, *Geography of a Horse Dreamer*. The latter full-length play contains some similar ideas, (geographical displacement), and techniques, (such as trance and possession states), with a different, albeit highly developed, dramatic structure.

Shepard's next play was another one act, *Little Ocean*, which opened March 26, 1974, at the Hampstead Theatre Club in London. *Little Ocean* was originally written for his wife at the time, O-Lan, and two other actresses, Dinah Stabb and Caroline Hutchison, on the perils of womanhood, dealing with men, and pregnancy. As Don Shewey notes, *Little Ocean* is a "real curiosity" for Shepard; it is the only play he's ever written for an all-woman cast (96). Shewey goes on to state that *Little Ocean* is especially significant because Shepard has often been accused of putting women in a subservient or objectified role when they appear in his plays with their male counterparts. (See Auerbach's essay in this volume.)

Years ago, all attempts to retrieve a copy of *Little Ocean* from Shepard, the Hampstead Theatre Club or his agent, proved fruitless. According to Shewey, "whether because it was written for a specific occasion or because it doesn't fit in with his manly image as a playwright, Shepard refuses to publish it or allow further performances" (96). Irving Wardle's review of *Little Ocean* might provide the best description of what the play was about:

> We start with a scene for the two friends, one tuning a guitar, the other practicing smoke rings. "Where did the habit come of handing out cigars?" "It's a tradition: Musta' [sic] come from Cuba." With that, the play takes off in a series of riffs—shadow boxing automobile

fantasies—before the pregnant Ms. Stabb lumbers in trailing a chair
and gloomily barricaded behind a newspaper.

The trio then get down to business. The horrors and pleasures of
parenthood come into focus in a series of internal sketches that convert
the players into warring parents, giggling teenagers, Eve and the
snake. (Wardle 29)

Although this is only one perspective of the play, it is one of the
few available. To this day, *Little Ocean* remains one of Shepard's lost
plays.

Shepard's fascination with Christopher Marlowe's *The Tragicale
History of Doctor Faustus* is well known: "You know [sic] Doctor
Faustus by Christopher Marlowe? I'd love to make a film of that
sometime. I'd even [sic] prefer it to Goethe's version because of
Marlowe's incredible language" (Cott 170). In 1975, during the same
year *Action* and *Killer's Head* opened, Shepard was commissioned for a
thousand dollars by the Mark Taper Forum to write an adaptation of
Doctor Faustus (Shewey 107). Although Shepard wrote the play, it
remains unpublished and unproduced to this date. The reason for the
Taper's decision not to stage *Doctor Faustus* is left to speculation,
which might be ventured by reading *Man Fly* ("a play, with music, in
II acts"), "adapted from Christopher Marlowe's 'Doctor Faustus.'"
Shepard describes this unpublished play as a "2nd draft," which is
written by hand on the title page of the play.

Shepard attempts to create an epic sense of visualization for *Man
Fly*. The action of the play takes place against a breathtaking backdrop
"of rocky mountains with snowy caps, in color, which can be
heightened or diminished-surrounding upstage in semi-circle" (*Man Fly*
1). There are also very high and low stage levels with a primitive room
below the mountain, Right Center. Although the setting helps
establish an epic atmosphere, Shepard's attempt to write allegorical
characters as the twentieth century equivalent of Marlowe's is an
experimental failure, however interesting.

Shepard's Doctor Faustus character, Skeetz, is a burnt-out poet in
search of the muse, instead of a frustrated scientist in search of the
secrets of the universe. Like Faustus, Skeetz sells his soul to the
Devil's emissary, Moustafo. Two angels, Billy Lee and Jackson
Hooker, look like "poets." They evoke Shepard's interest in baseball by
playing catch after they try to talk Skeetz into following their leader,

God. Once Skeetz signs the pact, "Man Fly" is inscribed in blood on his arm by the Devil.

Skeetz goes on to become a world famous evangelist, preaching, healing the sick and demanding donations for a period of twenty-four years. This only adds to the declamatory nature of the action, as many of the characters spend a great deal of time engaged in long speeches where they talk *at* the audience and each other rather than communicate with each other. In fact, there is very little conflict attempted throughout the structure of the play.

In *Man Fly*, Shepard also uses music and song as an effective device to underscore an emotional atmosphere which, on occasion, reaches the religious fervor of a church service:

> SKEETZ: DOES GOD HAVE POWER TO CURE A SINNER!
>
> *A loud fervent chorus in answer to him is heard over the P.A. behind the audience.*
> CHORUS: OH YES HE CAN!
> SKEETZ: DOES GOD HAVE THE POWER TO CURE THE SICK!
> CHORUS: OH YES HE CAN! (*Man Fly* 47)

Toward the end of *Man Fly*, Skeetz's own arm with the bloody inscription "Man Fly," is delivered to him. Faced with a certain future in Hell, Skeetz finally realizes what the inscription means:

> 'Man Fly!' Now I know the meaning of it. Now it strikes me plain as day! I had the chance to soar and now it's gone! Oh God! All I wanted was to love America! But I turned it on myself! LOVE MYSELF SKEETZ! LOVE MYSELF! (*calls out to himself as though it were another person*) SKEETZ! (*Man Fly* 55)

As a poet, Skeetz achieved recognition and self-awareness by writing with his arm. Skeetz's realization that he can be his own person and fly as an independent poet-artist comes not out of the dramatic action, but out of a view of his own arm, or himself. This could be viewed as a rather weak dramatic device used to help the character to discover himself, rather than Shepard's possible attempt to use symbolism about self-discovery. Nevertheless, once Shepard has established the self-discovery, there is no real attempt on Shepard's part to create any sort of climax other than a compelling visual ending.

The final moments of *Man Fly* seem to wind down with falling action. After one final speech by Skeetz, the mountains literally bleed red and Lucifer appears with his henchmen to take Skeetz away. The Devil kicks Skeetz's arm and comments ironically:

> Now see what's left. If I weren't the Devil I could be moved by bones. (*Looks up at mountains, speaks to them*) Mountains. You watch without a heart. (*He turns and stares at audience*). (*Man Fly* 60)

Although *Man Fly* was never produced, the story element of the artist selling a soul for success reappeared in Shepard's very next play, *Angel City* (1976). Shepard also experimented with a ten minute cowboy opera he wrote with Katherine Stone, *The Sad Lament of Pecos Bill on the Eve of Killing His Wife* (1976). Shepard then wrote *Suicide in B-Flat* (1976), which expanded on an old Shepard theme: the artist/hero as trapped by himself and society.

However in his next play, *Inacoma*, Shepard ventured into new territory related to society's experience of dealing with a comatose patient, as well as a well-established Shepard interest: the trance state from the point of view of the patient herself.

According to Shepard, he began writing a version of *Inacoma* as early as 1974. However, Shepard was unable to develop his idea into a fluid written structure:

> All I could visualize was a hospital bed. The coma victim and creature-characters. Then various scenes would start popping up, all out of context and wandering in and out of different realities. The scenes were joined by sounds of breathing, then [sic] music [sic] then back to sounds. I kept abandoning the idea of even starting to write something because the subject became too vast and uncontrollable. (Shepard, "Director's Statement")

In 1977 Shepard received a Rockefeller Foundation grant which enabled him to approach *Inacoma* from a more experimental point of view. Indeed, one reason why *Inacoma* might remain unpublished is due to the fact that the play was developed with and for a specific "company" of actors and musicians Shepard had worked with at the Magic Theatre in San Francisco. These were actors and musicians who had appeared or played in such plays as *Action*, *Killer's Head* and *Angel City*. Shepard describes the eclectic developmental process at the time:

> The main written material is in the form of songs. I've tried to make
> use of every influence that has moved me. From vaudeville, circuses,
> the Living Theatre, the Open Theatre, and the whole world of Jazz
> music, trance dances, faith healing ceremonies, musical comedy,
> Greek tragedy, medicine shows, et cetera. (Shepard, "Director's
> Statement")

Shepard is said to be highly interested in various states of consciousness, particularly in trance states. Although *Inacoma* is ostensibly based on the real-life case of comatose patient Karen Ann Quinlan, Shepard makes it clear that her case was "only a catalyst for our own discoveries." (Shepard, "Director's Statement")

Shepard worked on *Inacoma* with his actors and musicians for approximately six weeks. The company created a piece which the press called a "work in progress" when it opened at the Magic Theatre's Ft. Mason location on March 18, 1977. As the only remaining record of the play, the unpublished "script" is a thirteen page outline of the production divided into several separate picaresque scenes/songs dealing with the comatose patient, Amy Renfrow. Shepard also cites the actual names of the actors playing some of the characters in the play, such as "John" (John Nesci) and "Jane" (Jane Dornacker).

In order to give a different perspective on the patient herself, as well as the various officials and family members revolving around Amy, Shepard titles each scene separately with such subjects as "Shock/Trauma Unit," "Family Grieves" and "Experts Wake Up." In his review of the play, Bernard Weiner described the last scene: "Finally, her caricatured parents decide to pull the plug on the life/support machine, which brings Amy to sing her final lament: 'without seeing my being, they decide my fate'" (Weiner 15). In the outline of the play, "EXCUSES" shows this final scene in its seminal structure:

> *EXCUSES*—ensemble
> -each character cops out
> -machine forms—musicians joining machine
> -Amy grows stronger—rises
> -Mother and Amy see each other
> -Mother pulls plug
> -machine dies—silence
> -Amy starts breathing again.

SONG: "Breathing forever"—Ensemble
-pause with solo breath
-characters move off
-Mother/Amy alone
-music ends
-Mother/Amy breathe a capella (*Inacoma*)

Due to the fact that the play was developed with and for an ensemble of actors/musicians, that it was viewed as a "work in progress," and that the play is only available in outline form, it is no wonder that *Inacoma* remains one of Shepard's lost plays.

The next unpublished play by Shepard in this writer's possession is clearly one of the most amazing lost treasures he has written. After Shepard wrote *Curse of the Starving Class,* his dramaturgy would never be the same. Nevertheless, during this period Shepard also went through, according to Shewey, "one of the longest dry spells of his career" (124). Shewey lists three plays Shepard "started" during this period:

Freeway Life, about a character named Robin Ross who wants to move in with his friends Case, Frankie, and Ruby because he sees them as true artists; *Madagascar*, about two guys named Mack and Kinney in a hotel room; and *Links*, a play about golf (Shewey 124).

Interestingly enough, a play which Shepard starts that Shewey doesn't mention is *Jackson's Dance*: an elliptical combination free-form Jazz piece and "Action Painting" on the life and times of Jackson Pollock.

Jackson's Dance was reportedly to open sometime during the 1977–78 season at Joseph Papp's Public Theatre in New York. The play was to feature a director, Jacques Levy, and an actor, Kevin O'Connor, both of whom had worked on earlier Shepard one acts. Perhaps partly due to the fact that it never opened, the extant script has "*Incomplete—not to be published or even circulated*" in Shepard's handwriting on the cover. There are a number of places in the script where Shepard has written himself notes as to additions, deletions and re-editing ideas. All of the above notwithstanding, *Jackson's Dance* remains one of Shepard's most quintessential quests into new artistic territory.

It has been known for a long time that Shepard is influenced by Jackson Pollock and his style of "Action Painting." Even Shepard's statement that "I'm pulled toward images that shine in the middle of junk" (Vinson 697) proves his interest in Abstract Expressionism. His canon is replete with settings which look like or develop into large Action Paintings of the *mise en scène*. Shepard specifies his technical demands in his plays, (settings, lights, props and costumes), to create large art installations or sculptures. His *mise en scène* often transforms as the action of the play ensues to create a new visual design to the stage. *The Unseen Hand, Cowboy Mouth, Curse of the Starving Class, Buried Child,* and *True West* all share this idea. In *Jackson's Dance,* however, Shepard takes Pollock's idea of a large entropic Action Painting literally.

The play opens with a "Prelude" featuring a Native American woman, Uvavnuk, center stage next to a large blank canvas. She draws a large Thunderbird with colored sand as she chants and sings a song. After she leaves the stage, the sand painting is left for the actors to trample on with their blocking movements throughout the rest of Act I: "As the action continues the symbol is destroyed by movement, making another kind of picture by the end of the act" (*Jackson's Dance* 1).

Despite the fact Shepard eschews overly intellectual pursuits in the analysis of his plays, he freely uses what he calls a "Bibliography of Influential Sources" to investigate the following areas: (1) Jackson Pollock's life; (2) Pollock's criticism and his approach to painting; (3) Pollock's connection with the unconscious Native American Mythos as a cowboy from Cody, Wyoming; and (4) the Surrealists and their relationship with Pollock. Ideas are freely interpolated from a list of six books, including Francis V. O'Conner's *Jackson Pollock* and T. C. McLuhan's *Touch the Earth: An Anthology of French Poets from Nerval to Valéry.*

Shepard roughly follows Pollock's life from his early years as a young man in Cody, Wyoming, to the moment he is established as an artist in New York. Dreams and nightmares from some of his famous drawings appear as large paintings, and eventually become characters who are interpolated between the scenes. For example, in one scene Shepard makes three of Pollock's famous plates from his "Psychoanalytic Drawings": the Bird Monster (Plate #64), the Bull Demon (Plates #62 and #8) and the Horse Demon (Plates #79 and 49). They appear at Pollock's mother's funeral and insist that the artist sacrifice himself for a captured Indian brave. In a strange and frightening scene, the language is eerily dream-like:

BIRD: Qui qui achachacha! That's a heart. Give a heart Jack.
                 Dig it out. Dig a bloody heart. A sacka. A sacka.
                 Sacrifice. Sacka.
JACKSON: Not me yet! Not me! Not me yet! Ma! Look!
SNAKE: Oooh. sala. Sala. Sala. Winged. La, la, la. Bla, bla.
                 Sa, Sa. (*Jackson's Dance* 18)

Shepard also uses Jazz motifs, including music from Charlie
Parker, Fats Waller and Jimmy Yancey, between scenes to support the
atypical structure of the play. Indeed, Shepard's dramatic structure also
includes sequences in which Pollock is confronted by the Surrealists as
to whether he is continuing the artistic process which they began.
Pollock is also hounded by a chorus of critics; Shepard goes out of his
way to satirize their aesthetic theories. Finally, after Tricia Graham has
agreed to show Pollock's work in her gallery, the artist is "discovered"
by the critic Clement Greenberg. Shepard has Greenberg appear as a
ringleader in a circus. He presents Jackson as a brilliant, although
captured, artist:

GREENBERG: Ladies and gentlemen! *The* most powerful painter
             in contemporary America and the only one who
             promises to be a major one is a Gothic, morbid and
             extreme disciple of Picasso's Cubism and Miro's post-
             Cubism, tinctured also with Kandinsky and a dash of
             Surrealism! Look at this fella move! (*Jackson's Dance*
             52)

Shepard often defends his attitude that "resolutions" are too
contrived. The playwright should end the play where and when he wants
to. *Jackson's Dance* ends on an almost arbitrary note. Pollock attends
his final gallery opening under the sponsorship of Tricia Graham.
Graham introduces Pollock to a new potential sponsor, society matron,
Betsy Palmer. Pollock is so put off by the "art scene" that he gets
drunk and ends up insulting Palmer in front of the entire gallery
opening. The intelligentsia eventually leave as he is left alone with his
wife, Lee. In a speech which is reminiscent of Skeetz's final moments
on earth in *Man Fly*, Pollock is afraid of dying:

I'm scared now. Something's leaving my body. The Holy Ghost.
Right here in an art gallery. I DON'T WANT TO SEE THIS! Not
Now! I'm just comin into my own. I got my work to do, okay. I'll

make a deal. Just give me some time. Just a little more time. Then you can have me. (*Jackson's Dance* 62)

Although Shepard called *Jackson's Dance* "incomplete," the ending leaves the reader with the impression that Pollock was just another misunderstood and victimized artist on a drunken rampage in fear of dying before "time." We are left with the image of an angry artist, rather than a spiritual visionary who sought a different level of being through his art. Thus, despite the fact that the play isn't finished, Shepard never reaches a conclusion as to who the man Pollock was or what his art was all about.

In July of 1978, as *Buried Child* was opening, Shepard participated in the Padua Hills Writer's Conference. While he was instructing aspiring playwrights, Shepard wrote an unpublished monologue. Performed outside, *Red Woman* concerns a man with a madonna complex. He visits a large Mexican red stone statue, or "red woman," called Teresa and begs her to give him the location of a "treasure." He starts with something he hopes any saintly woman would believe:

You should know I'd marry you if I could. It's just that right now I need to get ahold of some cash. A little nest egg. Well ya'see what I mean? All you gotta do is give me a hint. Just a couple a'clues. I'll take it from there. "Whad'ya'say?" (*Red Woman* 1)

The man eventually tries other tactics to get information about the treasure he so desperately seeks. He apologizes, uses sentiment and hits on something that seems to work:

We could establish a nation, Teresa. Think of it. A whole nation. Invisible to the world. Only we would know. Just the two of us. Absolutely impenetrable. (*Red Woman* 3)

Jules Aaron describes what this looked like on the night of the festival:

In the last sequence, as the mournful sounds of a fiddle emerge from the darkness, image and environment blend—the Man and statue seem one, bathed in intense red light. (*Red Woman* 3)

The unpublished voice-over monologue for *Jacaranda,* "(a dance) (1979) written for Daniel Nagrin," is interesting. Performed prior to Shepard's collaboration with Joseph Chaikin, *Tongues* and *Savage/Love,* opened at the Public Theatre, the thirty minute dance piece features a barrel-house blues piano underscoring a voice-over monologue, as danced by Nagrin. It is the story of man who wakes up in his lover's bed and finds she is gone. At first he is seemingly unconcerned about his lover's absence and denies that he is a prisoner of Jacaranda's love. By the end of the monologue an interminable list of "I Need's" belies his imprisonment: "I need you now in the flesh. I need you now" (*Jacaranda* 4).

Red Woman and *Jacaranda* are not the most complex of Shepard's plays or monologues. (They certainly take Shepard full circle in the search for Shepard's "lost" plays.) Although they obviously show Shepard's maturity, they also reify Shepard's earlier one acts in which he experimented with small but imaginative images: *Cowboys, Up to Thursday, Dog* and *The Rocking Chair.*

That experimentation continues with *Blue Bitch,* a preparation for *Geography of a Horse Dreamer.* Both *Man Fly* and *Inacoma* experiment with trance and possession states and spirituality in a more spectacular way than *Red Woman. Man Fly* is an interesting, albeit experimental adaptation of Marlowe's *Doctor Faustus.* The story of the artist selling his soul for success becomes an idea Shepard used in writing his very next play, *Angel City.* The success or failure of *Inacoma* is dependent upon Shepard himself experimenting with a group of specific dedicated actors and musicians.

The most outstanding "lost" Shepard play, in this writer's opinion, rests with the unfinished *Jackson's Dance.* Despite Shepard's "incomplete" claims, the allegorical characters which work partially in *Man Fly* are used very effectively in *Jackson's Dance.* Even similar themes in both plays, (in this case the artist who is trapped by society and struggles to go beyond the known parameters of the material world), seem to be developed from *Man Fly* to *Jackson's Dance.* Therefore, Shepard continually uses experimentation by beginning plays he never finishes, writing complete practice plays, and writing monologues based on small images. The purpose of these experiments obviates the need to publish or release these "lost" plays to anyone.

As Shepard develops his dramaturgy with his experimentation, he is apparently not concerned about his lost plays, both finished and unfinished, being left behind or thrown away. The resultant later plays contain ideas from his lost plays and continue to generate Shepard's stated intention to "make sense out of nonsense." (Vinson 697). Finally, Shepard rejects the notion of critical interpretation in a similar way Jackson Pollock did with his Action Paintings:

> My plays have rarely been seen by critics for what they are but mostly for what they "represent." If they speak to Americans it's only because I happen to be American. I don't want to rid myself of my Americanism but to purge it through my writing. To go all the way through it and into a world which is totally alien and unrecognizable. It's that world that pulls me every time I write and it's [in] that world that writing holds its magic. Without it a theatre piece is nothing more than a representation of life without being a life of its own. (Shepard letter 2)

The overview of Shepard's "lost" plays has allowed us to witness the experimentation of a playwright trying to discover a new world that is totally alien and unrecognizable; a world that ultimately defies explication, other than the experience of Shepard's powerful journey into the flesh and blood of theater.

References

Albee, Edward. "Theatre: Icarus's Mother," *Village Voice*, Nov. 25, 1965, p. 15.

Chubb, Kenneth, ed. "Metaphors, Mad Dogs and Old Time Cowboys," *Theatre Quarterly*, 4.15 (1974).

Cott, Jonathan. "The *Rolling Stone* Interviews Sam Shepard," *Rolling Stone* 490, (1987).

Shepard, Sam. *Blue Bitch* (unpublished typescript).

———. "Director's Statement," Magic Theatre Press Release, Feb. 24, 1977.

———. *Dog* (unpublished typescript).

———. *Inacoma* (unpublished typescript).

———. *Jacaranda* (unpublished typescript).

———. *Jackson's Dance* (unpublished typescript).

———. Letter to Patrick Fennell (unpublished) written May 7, 1972.

———. *Man Fly* (unpublished typescript).

———. *Red Woman* (unpublished typescript).

————. *The Rocking Chair* (unpublished typescript).

————. *Up to Thursday* (unpublished typescript).

Shewey, Don. *Sam Shepard: The Life, The Loves, Behind the Legend of a True American Original.* Dell Publishing, 1985.

Tallmer, Jerry. "Tell Me About The Morons, George," *New York Post*, Oct. 13, 1964, p. 33.

Vinson, James, ed. "Sam Shepard" in *Contemporary Dramatists*. St. Martin's Press, 1973.

Wardle, Irving. "Fantasia on Childbirth," *The Times* (London), March 27, 1974, 18.

Washburn, Martin. "Cosmic Knockouts and a Mean Mama," *The Village Voice*, Jan. 25, 1973, p. 14.

Weiner, Bernard. "Stimulating Theatre Piece," *San Francisco Chronicle*, March 18, 1977, p. 15.

ICARUS'S MOTHER:
CREATIVE TRANSFORMATIONS
OF A MYTH

Albert E. Wilhelm

One of the least known figures in classical mythology is Naucrate, said to be the mother of Icarus. According to Robert Graves, Naucrate was a slave of King Minos of Crete. She met Daedalus and bore his son before Daedalus fell from favor and was imprisoned with this son in the Labyrinth (I, 312). Although Naucrate's mythological role provides the title for Sam Shepard's seventh play, the play itself contains no further reference to her and no specific allusions to the Daedalus-Icarus myth.

Among Shepard's early plays enigmatic titles like this one are hardly unusual. In fact, Richard Gilman has commented that titles like *Dog*, *Killer's Head*, *The Holy Ghostly*, *Shaved Splits*, and *Blue Bitch* often "appear as aggressions, put-ons, or parodies, but almost never as traditional titles in some direct or logical connection to the works" (xvii). He even claims that such titles suggest not literary works but rather "names of rock groups," scraps of graffiti, or isolated "writings on tee-shirts" (xvii). To be sure, the title *Icarus's Mother* is unconventional, but its connection with the text of Shepard's play is not entirely capricious. It does sound a note which helps viewers and readers to attune themselves to some important thematic concerns of the play. The various myths surrounding Daedalus and Icarus all focus on creative energy—its driving force to express itself and the opposing forces which attempt to repress it. The myths display a potential for fabulous achievements but also a corresponding possibility of failure and suffering. Shepard's play is a dramatization of these same forces in dynamic interaction.

In contrast to the flamboyant title, all the characters in *Icarus's Mother* have decidedly mundane names—Bill, Jill, Pat, Howard, Frank. From this cast of three men and two women, one has a difficult task in isolating any character who displays a clear parallel either with Icarus or with his more obscure mother. The most obvious candidate for the role of modern-day Icarus is, in fact, an unnamed, invisible character—the pilot who flies a jet plane above the picnic area where all the on-stage action occurs. At various points in the play this pilot circles above the earthbound characters, soars high into the sky, and ultimately falls into the sea in a fiery crash. The characters on the ground believe that the pilot is trying to make contact with them—to communicate by mysterious signals. When Jill asks, "Who would he be signaling to?," Howard promptly suggests, "His mother maybe. Or his wife" (64). If the Icarus-like pilot has only a remote presence in Shepard's play, then his presumed mother is even more distant. She exists only in the hypothesis of a single character, and Howard's impromptu speculation is never confirmed.

By means of his odd title and the snippet of dialogue from Howard—by giving top billing to Naucrate rather than to Daedalus—Shepard suggests a refocusing of the Icarus myth. Most earlier treatments of the story deal almost exclusively with the male characters—with relationships between fathers and sons. Traditionally we are invited to view Daedalus as the fabulous artificer who frees his son from the Labyrinth and offers him sound advice. Icarus is typically seen as the tragic victim of *hubris* because he is unwilling or unable to follow that advice. Embedded within the old myth, however, are the elements of a contrary interpretation. In this alternative reading Daedalus is not the saviour of his son but rather the son's arch-rival. Toward his son the father figure projects not creative energy but the forces of repression.

This antagonistic relationship between Daedalus and Icarus is prefigured by the antecedent story concerning Daedalus and his nephew Talos. Since Talos had been apprenticed to Daedalus, Daedalus stood in a paternal relationship to his nephew. In this case, however, the twelve-year-old student soon outdistanced his teacher. By making a saw from the jawbone of a serpent, by inventing the potter's wheel and the compass, Talos provoked the intense jealousy of his master. To preserve his own reputation, Daedalus destroyed his rival by luring him to the top of Athene's temple on the Acropolis and then pushing him over the edge. Thus, instead of being a mentor who fostered Talos's creativity, Daedalus was a jealous guardian of his art. In attempting to justify his act of murder, Daedalus claimed that Talos might have been involved in an incestuous relationship with his mother. The superimposition of this quasi-Oedipal conflict on the conflict between master and apprentice reveals that Daedalus opposed creative impulse on all fronts. Like the *senex iratus* in classical comedy, he felt compelled to block the erotic aspirations of a younger generation just as he thwarted its creative impulse.

Since Daedalus killed his nephew by pushing him from a high place, the death of Talos displays obvious parallels with that of Icarus. Daedalus's treatment of his own son is, of course, less overtly brutal. Nevertheless, we should pay careful attention to certain details of the escape from the Labyrinth. In this central story of the myth, Daedalus presumably speaks words like these: "My son, be warned! Neither soar too high, lest the sun melt the wax; nor swoop too low, lest the feathers be wetted by the sea. . . . Follow me closely . . . do not set your own course" (Graves I, 312–313). If the spirit of this paternal advice is good, its substance is surely deadly. The father has given his son a great gift but has also rigidly restricted the use of that gift. In prescribing a safe mean, he dictates inevitable artistic doom. Contrary to Daedalus's command, the artist cannot continually walk in the footsteps of his predecessors. To do so would be to produce nothing but clichés. As Harold Bloom has pointed out, powerful creators "wrestle with their precursors, even to the death," in order to "clear imaginative space for themselves" (5).

Implicit in the Icarus myth, then, is the notion that the life of the artist is a continual battle against the father or those who stand in the position of father. Interestingly enough, myth assigns no clear father to Daedalus. As a powerful creator he has transcended the limitations represented by the paternal figure, and he exists in myth never as child but exclusively as parent. Robert Graves suggests, on the basis of etymological evidence, that *Daedalus, Talos,* and *Icarus* may all be "different titles of the same mythical character" (I, 315). If this is the case, the three characters represent the artist at different stages of development. Daedalus is the mature artist who has escaped the heavy influence of the past while both Talos and Icarus are the aspiring artist fixed forever in myth at the moment of failed rebellion against the father.

I do not claim that Sam Shepard is a careful student of classical myth. Whether or not he actually knows the small details of the Daedalus story, his life and his plays happen to be full of diverse embodiments of the same mythic materials I have been discussing. Indeed, the Sam Shepard who has become a famous dramatist and actor is, in a very real sense, no longer his father's son. Born Samuel Shepard Rogers, Jr., Shepard has, by changing his name, literally escaped the stamp of identity placed on him at birth. In fact, Shepard has rewritten the history of his own nativity. In *Hawk Moon* he gives a lyric account which, according to Ron Mottram, greatly embellishes the "simple, prosaic facts" of his birth (2). From the beginning Shepard's plays have also been thickly populated by young males who attempt to create roles which give them independence from their fathers. Mottram describes Shepard's first play (*Cowboys*) as an expression of "youthful energy and role-playing" and his second (*The Rock Garden*) as a "rebellion against his past" (9, 11). As he grew beyond his literal father, Shepard also pushed past his predecessors in the theater. Iconoclastic both in his texts and his techniques, Shepard "has altered the conventions of theater as radically as Brecht or Beckett. . . . His work is based on . . . the refusal to be confined by inherited cultural or intellectual forms" (Wetzsteon 6).

If Daedalus is inherently an oppressor in the myth, why does Shepard's title focus on the mother of Icarus? Except for the obviously unflattering references in *Blue Bitch* and *The Sad Lament of Pecos Bill on the Eve of Killing His Wife*, no other Shepard title makes any mention whatsoever of females. Indeed, Shepard has been condemned as a sexist writer whose male characters "outnumber and overwhelm females," reducing them to the role of "domestic caretakers" (Falk 96). Bonnie Marranca asserts: "There is no expression of a female point of view in any of Shepard's plays." Shepard, she says, "is not simply traditional in his view of women, but downright oppressive" (30–31). Like the other plays, *Icarus's Mother* is certainly no paean to femininity, but it does remind us of an elemental symbolic opposition. Throughout history the paternal figure has typically symbolized authority and aggressive power while the maternal has suggested fertility and nurture. Quite naturally, then, the Muse is almost always portrayed as feminine, and clichés like "the mother of invention" show that this basic symbolism is deeply ingrained in our everyday habits of thought and speech. If *Icarus's Mother* is a play about creative energy, then its title identifies the symbolic character who should nurture it. By choosing a mythological character who is so obscure and by making her presence in the play so remote, Shepard is dramatizing the inaccessibility in contemporary society of the spirit which fosters creativity.

With this understanding of the complexity of the Icarus myth, let us now give more specific attention to Shepard's text. Although Shepard gives his work a title from mythology, the myth is not automatically a key to the play. Shepard's characters cannot be mechanically paired up with the individual figures in the myth. Michael Smith, director of the first production of *Icarus's Mother*, says that when he first read the play he "couldn't tell the characters apart" (26), and Shepard himself has commented that his notion of character is more fluid than that of traditional dramatists. Through his work with the Open Theater, he was schooled in the technique of "transformations"—a series of exercises in improvisation in which an actor in quick succession creates diverse characters in totally distinct contexts. In a note to the actors of *Angel City*, Shepard writes: "Instead of the idea of a 'whole character' with logical motives behind his behavior which the actor submerges himself into, he should consider instead a fractured whole with bits and pieces of characters flying off the central theme. Collage construction, jazz improvisation. Music or painting in space" (quoted in Gilman xiv). Such a comment (itself drifting off into elliptical constructions) applies just as readily to the characters in *Icarus's Mother*. No single character in the play can be identified with Icarus or with his father. Instead each character displays, at least momentarily, the creative impulse we identify with Icarus. At the same time, all these characters, individually and collectively, display those restrictive forces which limit creativity.

Shepard's play begins with all five of its characters distributed around the stage in a rigid geometric pattern. Four characters are placed at the corners of a square, and the fifth is in the center. All lie in exactly "the same position" (63), and at first all are totally immobile. Also on stage are a still smoking barbecue grill and "the remnants of a huge meal" (63). By means of this stiff tableau, Shepard provides both social and aesthetic commentary. He suggests that his characters have been totally passive consumers rather than creative producers. Although the stage is covered with lush green grass, the atmosphere is surely mechanical and restrictive rather than organic and fertile.

From this tableau emerges a brief non-verbal overture. Before the stage lights come up, the audience hears for some time the harmonious sound of birds chirping. This music from nature is followed by total silence and then by the noises of all the people on stage "belching at random" (63). Such belches are the obvious result of over-consumption, but they may also represent rudimentary attempts to communicate. Shepard's characters can emit elemental noises; they can seldom articulate meaning.

With their first actual words the characters comment on the vapor trails left by the jet plane above them. Pat wants to believe that the pilot has created a pattern—that the wispy white lines are actually skywriting. The others soon assert, however, that the "long stream of cloud is just excess gas" (64). Through this choice of words Shepard invites us to view the trail left by the Icarus-like pilot as a parallel to the sequence of belches heard earlier from the picnickers. Both can be construed as efforts to communicate, but both remain random and void of meaning.

In their mixed attitudes toward the jet pilot, Shepard's characters quickly display their "fractured," volatile natures. To some extent all of them identify with him and want to share the belief that he has achieved something notable. At the same time they are jealous of his high-flying antics and determined to diminish his achievement. Aroused by the sight of the plane above them, each character in succession rises from his or her static, recumbent position. On this simple level the pilot has inspired the first real action of the play. In the game-playing which follows, Jill projects herself into the role of the pilot's creative partner by asserting that she is his wife. Caught up in this desire to be in some way united with the pilot, Pat soon claims that she, too, is married to him. These two wives are described as "ripe" and "juicy" (65), suggesting their readiness to participate immediately in the creative process. By throwing kisses and yelling to the pilot, the two women try to lure him down to earth, and all three male characters soon echo their entreaties.

When the pilot fails to respond, their mood starts to turn ugly. Pat, for example, calls him a "booby." In her speech the word still serves as a term of endearment, but, since it also means a foolish person or the lowest scorer in a game, it begins to have overtones of condemnation. The tone of the male characters becomes overtly threatening. Howard yells out: "We've got your wives, mister pilot! You'd better come down or we'll take them away!" (65). The "ripe juicy wives" are reduced to hostages—chattel to be possessed or commodities to be bartered in return for the pilot's obedience. Just as Daedalus rules over Icarus, they threaten the pilot with dire punishments unless he conforms to their expectations. As the pilot flies away, they all join in heaping abuse on him. Bill, for example, calls him a "rotten guy" (66) and condemns him for running out on his wives and hypothetical children. This brief dramatic improvisation serves as an allegory of society's treatment of the aspiring creator. While it may sometimes encourage the creative impulse, it can also severely punish the individual who does not conform to societal standards.

Although the pilot leaves, his influence on the other characters is by no means ended. He was described earlier as "probably a test pilot" (64)—one who explores unknown realms. His example has inspired all the characters to rise out of their lethargy, and he soon motivates a few of them to want to leave the safe haven of the picnic area and explore the larger world around them. Pat is the first to propose a walk down to the beach, but her suggestion provokes a paranoid reaction among the others. Just as they tried to control the actions of the pilot, they also want to rigidly restrict her behavior. In her attempt to expand consciousness, they see only the possibility that she might fall and be knocked unconscious. They are like overprotective parents who watch over a child taking its first uncertain steps. Alluding to two primal images of mystery, they warn that she might drown in the ocean or get lost in the forest. As Pat sits on the ground, the others "remain standing and close in on her, slowly forming a circle" (67). Thus Shepard creates a powerful theatrical image of social oppressiveness.

After Pat has been suitably subdued, Howard abruptly switches his allegiance and endorses the idea of walking away from the picnic site. Even though Howard never actually leaves the immediate area, he does enter imaginatively into the role of the jet pilot. In a lengthy speech which is clearly "more operatic than conversational" (Smith 28), he gives a lyric account of what one might see and feel while flying high above the earth. According to Bonnie Marranca, "Howard's imagination takes flight like the plane overhead" (24). His powers of empathy have made him a visionary. In the ordinary world one's vision is usually circumscribed, as demonstrated by the tight circle which encloses Pat. In the high-flying plane, says Howard, "there's something to look at all around you. . . . You have so much to see that you want to be able to stop the plane and just stay in the same position . . . looking all around" (69).

Howard's aria is followed by Pat's monologue on fireworks. Pat concedes that the possibility of failure is ever present for those who refuse to remain earthbound, but she emphasizes also the potential for spectacular success. Last year's fireworks, she says, were admittedly defective, "but that doesn't mean it will happen again this year. Besides . . . some of them were beautiful. It's worth it just to see one beautiful one out of all the duds" (71). Instead of a solitary artist, Pat portrays herself as a lone pyrotechnic engineer. If everyone else abandons the fireworks in disgust, she will remain to ignite the last one in the pile and admire its trajectory.

Although Pat was the first to suggest a walk on the beach, Frank is the one who actually explores it and reports back to Howard and Bill. Frank is impressed by the awesome purity of what he has seen, and, like a traveler returning from a fabulous land, he describes it with a tone of reverence. Eager to share his discovery with the other men, he proposes "an expedition or an exploration" so they can "find out what there is to know" (73). For Bill such an invitation is apparently a threat. Rather than admit that life contains any mystery, he prefers to huddle under the shelter of simplistic truths. In a stilted, encyclopedia-like passage, he stubbornly denies that "there's anything to know" about the beach. It is composed, he says, "of sand which is a product of the decomposition of rock through the process of erosion. Sand is the residue of this decomposition which, through the action and movement of tides controlled by the location of the moon in relation to the position of the other planets in the hemisphere, finds itself accumulating in areas which are known to us as beaches" (73). Under this barrage of facts, Frank's commitment to real insight begins to waver. His proposed "expedition" becomes merely a hike on the beach "with a nice group of friendly neighborly neighbors," and even this plan is dependent on the weather and "the cost of the baby-sitters involved" (73–74). At this point in the play Frank's speeches become hackneyed and repetitious, just as he himself becomes a slave to social convention. He is taken in by Bill's lies—that Pat and Jill have a secret to tell him—and virtually reduced to a giggling adolescent as he speculates about what this secret may be. His earlier dedication to finding "out what there is to know" degenerates to idle curiosity about a totally trivial matter.

After Frank goes offstage again, Pat and Jill return to report on their expedition to the beach. They describe their attempts to urinate while crouching on the sand. According to Jill they "were straining and groaning" but "neither one . . . could get anything out" (76). Language such as this suggests, of course, the pains of childbirth, but in this case nothing comes of their labors. The ripe, juicy wives do not become mothers. As they squat on the beach, however, the jet pilot returns and writes across the sky an emphatic message: "E equals MC squared" (76). At first this formula from modern physics may seem totally irrelevant to the issues at hand, but it is surely more than a throwaway absurdist joke. High above a barren land, the pilot proclaims the ultimate truth about energy. According to this formula the potential for power is present in all matter, but this great potential is seldom realized and never without loss of mass. Just as the release of nuclear energy (through fission or fusion) requires a cataclysmic change, so too does any successful display of human creative energy. The mathematical formula may be an affirmation of hope, but it is also a promise of pain for all who choose not to follow in the paths of their fathers.

Shepard ends his play with a grand apocalyptic vision. Having successfully written his message, the pilot falls like Icarus into the sea. His spectacular crash is described by Frank as "the nineteenth wonder of the Western, international world"—"a recognized world tragedy of the greatest proportion and exhilaration" (77). The conjunction of words like "tragedy" and "exhilaration" suggests an uncertain attitude toward the crash, just as we might have ambivalent feelings about the fall of Icarus. Ultimately the crash cannot be called either a triumph or a disaster. It contains elements of both but transcends either label.

I have noted that Shepard's early dramatic training was in the transformation exercises of the Open Theater. In this particular play he has produced some complex transformations of the Daedalus-Icarus story. As a matter of fact, a basic concern in much of Shepard's work is this process of transformation itself. Ross Wetzsteon observes that again and again Shepard's characters "attempt to find their true nature by adopting roles, by performing, by hoping to become . . . what they fantasize they are" (8). In individual families and in society as a whole, this struggle to forge a new identity may leave in its wake pain and confusion, but it remains a necessary struggle. The prominent psychiatrist Henry A. Murray has suggested that the Icarus syndrome is "a common pattern of character and behavior." Characterized by "the desire to rise above the crowd, intellectually or socially, and to be admired for doing so," it is one basic "mode of expression taken by individual rebellion, the revolt of the son against his father" (Shroder 55–56). Clearly this is a pattern which is very familiar to Shepard, and he portrays numerous reenactments of the old myth.

References

Bloom, Harold. *The Anxiety of Influence.* New York: Oxford, 1973.

Falk, Florence. "Men Without Women: The Shepard Landscape." *American Dreams: The Imagination of Sam Shepard.* Ed. Bonnie Marranca. New York: Performing Arts Journal Publications, 1981.

Gilman, Richard. "Introduction." *Sam Shepard: Seven Plays.* New York: Bantam, 1981.

Graves, Robert. *The Greek Myths.* 2 vols. Baltimore: Penguin, 1955.

Marranca, Bonnie. "Alphabetical Shepard: The Play of Words." *American Dreams: The Imagination of Sam Shepard.* Ed. Bonnie Marranca. New York: Performing Arts Journal Publications, 1981.

Mottram, Ron. *Inner Landscapes: The Theater of Sam Shepard.* Columbia: University of Missouri Press, 1984.

Shepard, Sam. *The Unseen Hand and Other Plays.* New York: Bantam, 1986.

Shroder, Maurice Z. *Icarus: The Image of the Artist in French Romanticism.* Cambridge: Harvard University Press, 1961.

Smith, Michael. "Notes on *Icarus's Mother*." *Five Plays by Sam Shepard.* Indianapolis: Bobbs-Merrill, 1967.

Wetzsteon, Ross. "Introduction." *Fool for Love and Other Plays.* New York: Bantam, 1984.

OFFBEAT HUMOR AND COMIC MYSTERY IN SHEPARD'S PLAYS: *LA TURISTA, THE UNSEEN HAND, THE MAD DOG BLUES,* AND *FORENSIC AND THE NAVIGATORS*

Elizabeth Proctor

The strength of Sam Shepard's plays may be his bizarre sense of humor. His plays mix comedy and tragedy, and the blend is realistic. Sometimes humor grows out of this realism, but often it results from incongruous situations or dialogue.

For example, in *La Turista*, it is absurd, yet undeniably amusing, when a boy bursts in unannounced on Salem and Kent and refuses to leave. Not only is this situation droll, but the boy's improbable dialogue reinforces the strangeness of the situation. After entering Salem's and Kent's room, the boy, supposedly a Mexican, takes off his pants, crawls into bed, and says, "What do you know about trouble, Mom?" (265). Occasionally the boy speaks Spanish; usually, though, he speaks informal English, and wonders such things as, "How do you score chicks on a horse?" (265). Sometimes his English is oddly

formal, as in the following speech which amuses the audience because
it is unlikely that the Mexican who referred to "scoring chicks" would
have spoken it, and because it is self-consciously about language at the
very time when Shepard is using the inconsistencies in the boy's own
language as a source of humor:

> The people in this area speak the purest Mayan existing today. The
> language has changed only slightly since the days of the great Mayan
> civilization before the time of the conquest. It's even more pure than
> the Mayan spoken by the primitive Lacandones, who live in the state
> of Chiapos. It's even purer by far than the Mayan spoken in the
> Yucatan, where much Spanish and Latino admixtures have been added.
> In short, it's very pure and nearly impossible for an outsider to learn,
> although many have tried (271).

This speech about purity of language is paradoxically spoken by a boy
whose own language could not be less "pure"; it is a very strange
mixture of styles which is clearly demonstrated in the following speech:

> The man here is the most respected of all, or I should say, his
> profession is. But then, we can't separate a man from his profession,
> can we? Anyway, there are several witchdoctors for each tribe and they
> become this through inheritance only. In other words, no one is
> elected to be a witchdoctor. This would be impossible since there is so
> very much to learn and the only way to learn it is to be around a
> witchdoctor all the time. . . . He listens carefully and watches closely
> to everything his father does and even helps out in part of the
> ceremony as you see here. A great kid (271).

The phrase "a great kid," completely out of keeping with the formal
tone of the rest of the speech, amuses an audience.

Yet the line between humor and pathos is not well defined in
Shepard's plays, and this is especially true of his use of incongruity—
which can be either ridiculous, and thus amusing, or a mirror of the
ambiguities of human nature, and thus painful. Communication rarely
occurs. Relationships are fragile to the point of absurdity. Witness the
end of Act One of *La Turista*, with its blend of tones:

> After hanging up the phone, the boy says: That's my father.
> Salem: Your father is dead. You're going with me. We have more
> things to do.

> Boy: That's the first time he ever speaks on a phone in his life. He says to start walking down the road toward my home and he'll start walking toward me, and we'll meet halfway and embrace.
> Salem: How will you meet in the dark: You can't even see the road.
> Boy: We'll meet in the light. My home is far from here. We'll meet as the sun comes up. We'll see each other from very far off and we'll look to each other like dwarfs. He'll see me, and I'll see him, and we'll get bigger and bigger as we approach.

The boy then explains he'll sing songs to his father. Salem counters, "Your father is deaf!" But the boy ignores him and continues his monologue:

> And we'll sit together and smoke by the side of the road until a truck comes by heading toward my home. And my father will kiss me good-bye and climb on the back and drive off, and I'll wait for another truck going the other way. A pale blue truck with a canvas back, carrying chickens and goats, and a small picture of the Madonna on the dashboard, and green plastic flowers hanging from the rear view mirror, and golden tassels and fringe around the window, and striped tape wrapped around the gear shift and the steering wheel, and a drunk driver with a long black beard, and the radio turned up as loud as it goes and singing Spanish as we drive out into the Gulf of Mexico and float to the other side.
> Salem: You'll never make it alive! (278–279).

Certainly there are bewildering alternatives here: your father is dead; your father is deaf; you and your father will die in your hut. The plan to drive out into the Gulf of Mexico and float to the other side is met by Salem's astute observation, "You'll never make it alive!" It might be argued that there is a certain humor underlying these statements, but if so, it is a cruel humor.

Another important aspect of Shepard's humor and one which occurs with some frequency in *La Turista*, is the joke inherent in alluding to bodily functions—that is, that man is a slave to his body, despite his alleged lofty intellectual pursuits.

It might be said that *La Turista* is based on this premise. The play opens with a discussion of ways to ease sunburn pain. Kent gives a very scientific description of how sunburn is acquired:

Well the epidermis is actually cooked, fried like a piece of meat over a charcoal fire. The molecular structure of the fatty tissue is partially destroyed by the sun rays, and so the blood rushes to the surface to repair the damage. (257)

Momentarily he digresses to more philosophical arguments. Kent says that he came to Mexico to disappear:

Salem: You came here to disappear?
Kent: That's right. Didn't you? To relax and disappear.
Salem: What would you do if you did disappear?
Kent: Nothing. I'd be gone.
Salem: I ask you that face to face. It deserves to be answered.
Kent: Do you know how soon you can start peeling it? (259)

And, at once, they are back to the apparently inescapable issue of sunburn. Without missing a beat, Salem answers, "Not before it's dead, I can tell you that much" (259). And an extended conversation about the proper peeling technique has begun. It should be noted that not only is the way Kent returns the focus from the abstract implications of disappearing to the concrete issue of sunburn amusing, which it is, but it is also realistic, especially in the way Salem immediately understands his question. Exchanges such as these represent the natural ebb and flow of conversation, and help to establish that these two people know each other well enough not to have to be specific about every allusion they make.

Soon, Kent becomes immobilized with dysentery and thus even less able to deal with the surprise invasion by the Mexican boy. Salem's and Kent's plight is reduced to absurdity: there is a naked Mexican in their bed and Kent is unable to leave the bathroom because, as he yells from behind the door, "I do have diarrhea after all!" (265). Throughout most of Act One, Salem attempts to cope with his illness and the presence of the Mexican, but Kent's only contribution is to proclaim from time to time that "It's getting looser!"

When he is finally, apparently, released from the grip of his affliction, his reaction is particularly amusing. The stage directions read, "Kent enters from the stage right door. . . . He crosses center stage, strutting":

> Kent: Well! I feel like a new man after all that. I think I flushed the
> old amoeba right down the old drain.
> Boy: Olé!
> Kent: Yes sir! Nothing like a little amoebic dysentery to build up a
> man's immunity to his environment. . . . And the old body ain't
> nothing without a little amoeba. (267)

Obviously, Kent's pride in his mastery of his own bodily functions
is amusing, especially since he is almost instantaneously laid low
again, literally, by the old amoeba when he faints at the end of this
speech. But as in the case of the other contradictions, the line between
the humorous and the pathetic is a fine one, not easily defined. Just as
we become accustomed to Shepard's use of the physical to represent
comic absurdity, we are reminded that, carried to its logical conclusion,
man's inability to master his physical nature ends in death. The
witchdoctor's beheading of live chickens and his sprinkling of their
blood on the prostrate form of Kent "runs straight toward the upstage
wall of the set and leaps right through it, leaving a cut-out silhouette of
his body in the wall" (300). The idea of disappearance which has been
discussed through the play, and as we have seen earlier was apparently
lightly treated—as when Kent comments to Salem on his reasons for
visiting Mexico: "You spend thousands of hours and dollars and plane
rides to get to a place for relaxation. To just disappear for a while. And
you wind up like this. With diarrhea . . . "(259)—becomes, at the
play's conclusion, an actuality which is frightening and threatening.
Literal disappearance. That Act Two supposedly takes place before Act
One does not change the stress on "personal negation" (to borrow from
Coleridge) but, if anything, strengthens the sense of mystery, loss of
control, and disorder which is a part of the theme.

The mixture of comedy and tragedy which typifies Shepard's work
makes his plays realistic in that life is seldom clear-cut and any one life
is bound to be a mixture of experiences, some good, some bad. At the
same time, Shepard's work is hard to categorize because he emphasizes
the inconsistencies of human existence by calling attention to man's
absurd situation—for example, longing to be intellectual and
philosophical; yet, in reality, being at the mercy of his own primitive
bodily functions.

Shepard's propensity for humor was obvious in his earliest works,
and from the start dialogue played an essential part in the creation of
comedy. In *The Unseen Hand*, the Morphan brothers have a distinct

country-western twang which contrasts with Will the space freak's more formal accent. When they meet, Willie proclaims: "I've traveled through two galaxies to see you. At least you could hear me out" (7). To this conservatively couched appeal Blue replies: "You been hittin' the juice or something? What's yer name, boy?" Also, just the idea of an encounter between a space freak and a nineteenth-century bandit is funny.

Here, as in the other plays discussed, Shepard's use of understatement is particularly amusing. Some of the lines between Blue and Cisco point out the discrepancy between the world of their childhood and the modern mechanized world. When Blue introduces Cisco to the concept of a car he explains that "some of 'em'll do over a hundred mile an hour."

> Cisco: What's that mean, Blue?
> Blue: That means in an hour's time if you keep yer boot stomped down on that pedal you'll have covered a hundred mile a territory.
> Cisco: Whooee! Sure beats hell out of a quarter horse, don't it? (16)

Later, when Blue is explaining that he's afraid of the law, Cisco asks him why he's "scared a' the law all of a sudden."

> Blue: It ain't so sudden as all that. I'm goin' on a hundred and twenty years old now. Thanks to modern medicine.
> Cisco: That a fact? Sure kept yerself fit, Blue (17).

Another source of humor is the difference between what members of the audience would consider a pleasant sort of pastime and what appeals to the Morphan Brothers. They've been lonely and are glad that they'll soon be reunited:

> Cisco: Well, before you know it we'll be back together just like old times. Robbin', rapin' and killin'.
> Blue: Yeah boy! (19)

The introduction of a revolution-talking cheerleader is inherently ludicrous. This particular cheerleader has been abused, though, and he's afraid of the kids from another school who beat him up. He's very intense, very anxious:

Kid: I'm never going to lead another cheer! Never! Not for them or anybody else! Never! Never! Never! Never! Never! Never! Never! Never! Never!
Blue: Atta boy. Get it out a yer system.
Kid: I'll just stay over near the drainage ditch there. I won't get in your way. I promise.
Cisco: Good.
Kid: If those Arcadia guys come by here don't tell them where I am, O.K.?
Cisco: O.K.
Kid: Oh, would you mind waking me up in the morning? I don't usually get up too easy. (21–22)

The unexpected intensity of "I'll never lead another cheer. . . Never! Never! Never! . . ." and "Oh, would you mind waking me up in the morning?" is extreme and regales the audience. Further, his repeated use of the word "never" sounds very much like the repetitive chants which characterize cheer-leading.

Although the play is amusing, it probes the serious topic of revolution. Shepard is alternately grave and satiric. For example, when Willie is trying to set up the Morphan Brothers to outwit the High Commission, he tells them in great detail about his plan and the layout of Nogoland where, Willie insists, "slaves work day and night under constant guard by the soldiers of the Raven Cult." When Blue asks about the identity of the "Raven Cult," Willie answers that they are "fierce morons cloaked in black capes" (32). Amidst all of the serious talk of insurrection, the concept of fierce morons cloaked in black capes puts a certain perspective on the permanence and importance of human social systems.

Another tactic for creating humor is to balance the everyday aspects of life, such as eating, against the extraordinary or the horrible. In the following passage, Shepard also uses understatement and the discrepancy between the dialects of Cisco and Willie to make the comedy even more emphatic:

Cisco: So ya' say this here Lagoon Baboon's an ornery critter, eh Willie?
Willie: Yes. Very ornery, as you say. He can eat three times his weight in human flesh in less time than it would take you to eat a donut. (34)

Yet another strategy used is the discrepancy between the seriousness of situation and the appearance and demeanor of the characters. A long debate occurs over whether the cheerleader should pull up his pants or not, whether he should be killed, and/or whether to allow him to preach revolution. Cisco and Blue are inclined to be lenient:

> Cisco: And pull up yer pants, fer Christ's sake. (The kid goes to pull up his pants.)
> Sycamore: I told ya' to keep yer hands raised.
> Kid: Well, I can't do both.
> Blue: Let him pull up his pants, Sycamore.
> Sycamore: This here is a spy in case you forgot. I say we plug him right here and now.
> Blue: And I say we let him pull up his doggone pants!
> Cisco: What do yu say, Willie?
> Willie: I have come to find any means possible to free my people. If he has information we should listen.
> Sycamore: O.K. But keep yer hands high, mister. (37–38)

The kid then begins a long and serious speech which seems ridiculous for someone whose pants are down. Moreover, a cheerleader is not expected, conventionally, to concern himself with such weighty issues, nor to be the advisor or leader or overthrower of outlaws:

> Kid: Ten to fifteen is all you'll need in the initial stages. It's important to remember that what you're organizing is more than a gang of bandits. Guerilla Warfare is a war of the masses, a war of the people. The guerilla band is an armed nucleus, the fighting vanguard of the people. It draws its great force from the mass of the people themselves. Bandit gangs have all the characteristics of a guerilla army: homogeneity, respect for the leader, valor, knowledge of the ground and often even good understanding of the tactics to be employed. The only thing missing is support of the people and inevitably these gangs are captured and exterminated by the public force. (38)

Obviously a dissatisfaction with society underlies this play, but the point that America is imperfect is made stronger rather than weaker by presenting it in humorous terms. Criticism moderated by humor is more effective because it is better received than extreme invective would be. When the Morphan Brothers look for help and want to go to the top person, they wonder if that might be the mayor, then decide that no, he runs the cops, the governor runs the mayor, congress runs the governor and the President runs the congress; we laugh because these unsophisticated hicks obviously don't understand our system. And also because they do.

Revolution was a popular topic in the sixties, and Shepard's concerns with social ills are thus not surprisingly reflected in his plays. Many of the same concerns and humorous tactics used in *The Unseen Hand* are used in a whole group of these early works. This is true as well of Shepard's bizarre myth-laden plays. While many critics of Shepard's work have reverently discussed his treatment of mythic subject matter—Richard Gilman, Bonnie Marranca, and others—I believe his treatment of myth is more often than not tongue-in-cheek, a kind of humorous exposé of scholarly legerdemain. Shepard himself has said, "By myth I mean a sense of mystery and not necessarily a traditional formula. A character for me is a composite of different mysteries. He's an unknown quantity. If he wasn't it would be like coloring in the numbered spaces ("Language," 55).

Keeping in mind Shepard's equation of myth and mystery, several general areas are represented in most of his plays. These areas are *art* (What is it? Where does it come from? What is an artist?), *identity* (the quest for roots), and *reality* (What is it?). Underlying these general concerns is the even broader issue of what it means to be human. Shepard explores or presents these concerns sardonically, not only through perverse dialogue, which he has said, for him, especially retains the potential for making leaps into the unknown, but also through weird staging (or the lack of it), and the improbable physicality of the actors. Laughter is just as important as pathos and sometimes more effective. Because it is so difficult, with Shepard, to break apart a play that only works as a unity, an examination of the oddly comic *The Mad Dog Blues*, from beginning to end, may be the most telling way of examining the way differing elements come together to produce a sense of mystery, and of clarifying Shepard's use of myth.

The prologue (which consists of two monologues) presents Kosmo and Yahoodi to the audience. Besides giving "facts" about each, the monologues underscore that paradox is to be the method of the play—paradox that is at various times amusing in a sad way and at other times merely sad. Kosmo, for example, "hates religion" but "asks for God's help." He "moves from spot to spot across the planet hoping to find a home." Yahoodi "prefers isolation" but "hates to be lonely." Obviously, then, language, the very first words spoken by the main characters, sets up two of the major concerns of the play—the search for roots, and the desire humans seem to have to define, although a person cannot, properly speaking, be defined. Yahoodi and Kosmo try to define themselves, often hilariously, and the tension that results from trying to do what is impossible forces paradox and, finally, has an opposite effect from the effect one assumes the characters intend—the audience assumes a sense of the *expansion* of human potential. Presumably, this *is* what Shepard intends.

For a play that takes place all across the globe, Shepard gives us an "open, bare stage. All the places the characters move through are imagined and mimed." Thus the audience will have to suspend disbelief even more than ordinarily is required in what is already an artificial situation, a play; there will be no props whose alleged task is to add a sense of reality. Also, we are told that "the play opens with the theme music which Kosmo keeps hearing throughout the play," music which "is heard at different times but not necessarily when Kosmo says he hears it in the script." So again, right from the start, is the concern, "What constitutes reality?" If the audience hears music when Kosmo doesn't and vice versa, when is the music really playing? The sense of mystery is heightened because sometimes the audience and Kosmo hear the music at the same time. Thus it is not even possible to say, "Well, Kosmo is a kook and it doesn't matter whether he hears music or not; it only is real when the audience hears it."

In the prologue, the third concern I mentioned—that of the nature of art and the artist—is only evident in Kosmo's and Yahoodi's appearances. Kosmo carries a conga drum, and his dress reveals that he is a rock-and-roll star; Yahoodi, his sidekick who is presented in the play as a lesser artist (if one at all), is dressed as a dope dealer and carries a flute. But the opening lines of the play proper bring into a sharper focus Shepard's concern with art. Kosmo tells Yahoodi that he's "had a vision" which came to him "in music."

> It was like old rhythm-and-blues and gospel, a cappella, sort of like
> The Persuasions but with this bitchin' lead line. Like a Hendrix lead
> line. Like a living Hendrix lead line right through the middle of it.
> (151)

Perhaps picking up on Kosmo's use of the word "vision," Yahoodi asks "what about the visuals? Did ya see any pictures?" and Kosmo responds: "A tall golden woman like Marlene Dietrich or something. In short shorts and teased blonde hair. Carrying a whip." At this point the stage directions read "she appears and cracks her whip." Yet neither Kosmo nor Yahoodi takes note of this physical manifestation of the vision.

The art is made real only in the sense that, as an audience, or as a reader, we are given an actual interpretation of the vision which still remains imaginary—as if we saw a painting of what an artists has imagined; we would not thus have the actual picture he saw, but rather a representation of it. But then Marlene comes down to the audience and sings "Jungen Mensch." Since this is much more specific than what Kosmo described, she begins, at this point, to seem real, to have a life of her own as much as is possible for a character in a play to have—and for a character carrying all the associations of the physical likeness and name of Marlene Dietrich.

Dietrich, Mae West, Paul Bunyan, Captain Kidd, and Jesse James add to Shepard's use of myth as mystery, since these characters fail to exactly duplicate those whom they are "supposed to." On the other hand, they also subtract from Shepard's use of myth as mystery since these are to an extent stock characters who instantly draw stock comic responses from the audience as a whole. There is a constant give and take and balancing off between these two uses of myth.

In the opening scene, Marlene's song appropriately reiterates the art theme. We don't know, really, where she or her song (or is it Kosmo's?) comes from; there is a search for reality, for roots:

Silly boys just young men
Go away and then they come again
They don't yet know who they are
Silly boys just young men following a star.

Loneliness and transience are companions; the young men are fools who "end and then begin and end again like reflections in a pool."

And loneliness comes like a dart
There's nothing to find till you find your heart. (151-52)

Here, thematically voiced, is Shepard's assertion that mind, body, and emotions are necessarily linked.

The main problem with Kosmo and Yahoodi is that this linkage has either broken down, or it has never fully developed. Their search for gold is a search for self, but perhaps it is not so obvious that the search is doomed to failure—what is needed most is *not* a search, but stability. Then mind, body and emotions could fall in together, in unity; as it is, treks through space and time virtually assure that the body will be one place, while mind and emotions will remain loyal to the latest and last place as home, with all the associations of home. Thus body and mind and emotions remain unsynchronized, one step (or more) out of tune with each other. This point is implicit early in the play when Yahoodi asks Kosmo, "How's your depressions?" Kosmo responds: "They come and go like the wind. Here today, gone tomorrow. If I could just put something together. I keep feeling like I'm getting closer and closer to the truth" (152). That truth can be found or owned is gradually seen as the ultimate mystery, and so is slowly revealed as the ultimate myth.

Paralleling the concern with that division of self is a concern with the division of people from each other. This is a frequent theme for Shepard, and is related to his interest in the problem of defining reality. Yahoodi says:

> Ever since I was a little boy I used to watch the subway come up out of the ground and wonder about all those people. Now all those people were just living their lives and couldn't care less about me. About how separate we were. Them on the train and me watchin' them. Them in their life and me in mine. I could see them and hear them and smell them but they didn't even know I existed. Good for them I'd say. Good for me. Hurray for life. (153)

An additional question raised by Yahoodi is that of the relationship between the perceiver and the perception, between the art and its inspiring vision. Appropriately, at this point Kosmo turns to Mae and observes: "You're much smaller than the image I have in my head of you. You seemed so big in the movies" (153). She doesn't much care about his destroyed image, or about anything except herself, and cynically remarks that "big surprises come in small packages." But he keeps trying to bring his vision into focus with reality; since he prefers the vision (and why not? he created it), he tries to change the way she really is:

Kosmo: I had this vision of you, and you were singing like Janis Joplin.

Mae West: Never heard of her.

Kosmo: She's dead.

Mae West: Maybe that's why.

Kosmo: She was a lot like you. Lots of balls. She could really belt it out.

Mae West: Yeah, well, beltin's not exactly my specialty. (153)

Trying to make Mae West in some way embody Janis Joplin is ridiculous, but also perhaps an effort to lessen the sad separateness between people. Later in the play, Waco claims to have the living Jimmie Rodgers within himself. Most of the time, though, the stress is on divisiveness, as when Kosmo tells Mae that the revolution's on, and she asks, "What channel?" Or when Kosmo's father doesn't recognize his own son. Or when Waco, in a friendly, down-to-earth style, drawls out: "Name's Waco. Waco Texas. That's where I was born." And Yahoodi replies: "Who gives a rat's ass?" The incongruity here is amusing, but the lack of communication is not.

The notion that everyone is alone becomes more pointed as the play progresses, and moves from the comic to the nightmarish. Even when asleep the characters are aware of loneliness; Captain Kidd wakes up screaming at one point and yells, "Every man for himself!" This dark vision becomes reality when they dump Waco, a nonswimmer, into the water in a mad dash to reach land in time to compete for gold. Selfishness and self-centeredness are the rule of the day. Yahoodi shoots Captain Kidd because he wants the treasure all to himself. Even lovers (or especially lovers?) are ultimately selfish. Paul Bunyan tells Marlene that he likes her ability to understand him; then only a few lines later when she comments on the "wonderful music" that sounds like "golden leaves" he responds, "I'm sorry, ma'am, but I don't hear nothin' but the breeze" (181). Finally, Marlene leaves Paul because she hears Yahoodi calling her like "my own voice. My own voice calling me back." And well might it be, for, like the lovers in *Evangeline*, "Marlene wanders off in search of Yahoodi, Yahoodi in search of Marlene, but they never meet. Paul tries to follow her but he gets lost" (190). This scenario extends to the other characters who "keep searching for each other but never meet, even though at times they may pass right by each other. They keep calling out each other's names." That such separation and loneliness is man's lot finds ultimate expression in Captain Kidd's final words: "Only I will know how I died. Only me. There'll be lies. There'll be legends. But only I will know" (192).

As I have tried to make clear, the balance of this strangely entertaining play focuses on the side of man's selfishness and separation. But it would be misleading to represent loneliness as the only alternative; if there were only division, division wouldn't be apparent. It is only before a background of reconciliation, of love and caring, of hearing, and of the notion that mankind (if not man individually) perhaps has one unifying mission, that separation is even apparent, perhaps welling up out of Shepard's fascination with "what it means, in real terms to die and be born again" (Chubb, 16). Captain Kidd, in the end, seems to be moving through his own individual death and on into the unknown:

> Where does the mind go? All the visions in space. All the things dreamed and seen in the air. Where do they go? Something flies away. I can see it flying. Taking off like a flamingo. Soaring higher and higher. A beautiful pink bird flying alone. Out over the everglades. Out over the swamps. Higher and higher, straight into the sun. If only I could sing. (192)

The artists mentioned in the play, especially Janis Joplin and Jimmie Rodgers, have perhaps sung for him. And so, in a sense, does Kosmo. Throughout he has, as he has vocally maintained, "opted for life", in juxtaposition to Yahoodi who shoots death into his own veins and literally kills Captain Kidd, and almost destroys the play, in that Shepard has Yahoodi nearly "cop out" before the play is over. Only because Kosmo urges him on does he keep going. To the "dead" Yahoodi, Kosmo comments:

> You can get up now. Come on. Look, it's not going to work out if you go and off yourself right when everything gets going so good. You just bring the whole . . . thing to a dead end. We got all these characters strung out all over the place in all these different lives and you just go and rub yourself out. What a . . . drag. Is that responsible? Now I ask you, is it? Yahoodi! If you don't want to go through with this thing then just tell me. Just come right out and tell me. But don't kill yourself off in the middle of the plot. (187)

They negotiate about whether to continue at all, or whether to continue together, but their communication, which seems to be the only real communication in the play, threatens to break down because, essentially, they view life from two very different angles. As Yahoodi says, "I'm struggling with something in me that wants to die!" And Kosmo replies, "And I'm struggling with something that wants to live" (189). They decide to separate because they cannot decide on a common definition of reality.

The question of who is in control of this play, who invented it, returns us to the beginning of Act One. It is Kosmo who speaks first and who tells Yahoodi that he has had a vision. After his second vision, of Mae West singing the blues like Janis Joplin, Yahoodi asks if he should come back.

> Kosmo: Not yet. I haven't been able to give it any form. She's just sort of strutting around. There's so much cigarette smoke you can hardly see her.
> Yahoodi: What's it like there?
> Kosmo: Full of inspiration! Jack Kerouac country! The Grateful Dead. The Airplane, Quicksilver. The air is full of grist for the mill.

Kosmo the musician is also Kosmo the artist and visionary, and the play with its authorial intrusions is also about the myth and the mystery associated with producing art and of being an artist. But much changes by the end of the play. Although Kosmo claims to choose life, his last words are words of despair: "I can't hear the music any more!" And Yahoodi, who has been presented as Kosmo's sidekick and the lesser artist of the two (at least Marlene calls him an artist), bows out of the play on an optimistic note: "You worry too much! Everything'll work out for the best!" Certainly this is a change from the Yahoodi who has predominated to this point, a struggler with something within himself that wants to die, and a dreamer of apocryphal visions—much to Kosmo's irritation. It is as if the two characters have exchanged points of view.

Perhaps the secret of Kosmo's trouble lies within a statement he makes early in the play, a response to Paul Bunyan's notion that nothing is like the North Woods for a little peace and quiet:

> But I'm a musician! I've got to create! I've got to get back to the city.
> Back to my band. Back to my roots. I've lost touch with my roots.
> (155)

Rootless and adrift, Kosmo has visions which take on a life of their own. And perhaps this is always the case. The vision is born in the artist, but it is part of something greater than him, and independent of him to the degree that it partakes of, and mirrors, something universal in origin. For the artist—the vessel—the "loss" of control or of a sense of direction can feel like disorientation or death.

From beginning to end, the play is about the need to establish and maintain a home base and a point of reference. Reality is presented as a chameleon, but at least if viewed before the background of stability, perceivable as a chameleon. In the prologue, Kosmo characterizes himself as "hoping to find a home." But he doesn't, at least not if the play is to be believed. In fact, none of the characters has a sense of permanence, not even Waco, who on the surface seems simple and sure of himself.

> Waco: Name's Waco. Waco Texas. That's where I was born.
> Kosmo: But look where it got you. You're from Texas?
> Waco: Born and raised.
> Kosmo: How'd you wind up here?
> Waco: I'm just here. That's all. I'm just here.

Even Waco seems to lose his sense of identity, finally feeling that he is really Jimmie Rodgers.

The play undermines the myth of love as a stable base, as the characters switch lovers with abandon when circumstances change. Shepard seems to display a rather cynical sense of humor on this point. Paul Bunyan, loyal to his ox, deplores his loss of Babe. Marlene replies, "It's hard to lose a loved one." "It's even harder to find one," he answers (159). Kosmo and Yahoodi have genuine feelings for each other, but they end up separated, and seeing the world in totally different ways. Mae West and Jesse James ride off together because he promises that his folks will treat her "like family." She suggests that all of the characters could go home together, and, indeed, the play ends with all of the characters singing "Home." Lest this be taken as an optimistic ending, the words to "Home" indicate not roots, but change—not arrival, but a journey:

> Home is like a rolling stone. . . .
> Home got no rules, it's in the
> Heart of a fool. (194)

If there is a permanent home, it would seem to be in death, or at least, in the weakening of artistic vision. Just before the curtain falls, the characters "join hands and dance and march together around the stage, through the audience, and out into the street." Yet they have perhaps launched something of themselves within the audience, a sense of wonder as to whether there is a perfect home, stability, nirvana. Shepard's answer is indefinite, but seems to emphasize the negative, at least in this life, for now.

Also, Kosmo's assertion that "now is real" (154) is brought into doubt by the shifting nature of both "now" and "real" throughout the play. The supposedly ephemeral ghost girl who was deployed by Captain Kidd in the seventeen-hundreds to guard his treasure loses a pitched physical battle with Marlene Dietrich and claims to be saving herself for Elvis. So the temptation to interpret the play by saying that Shepard holds out some kind of hope for an eventual, if heavenly, home, must also take into account the wandering ghost girl who was picked up in "some bar in Frisco." The motif of illness, given a physical dimension when Waco and Marlene are seasick, is one of the universals holding the characters together in his play-land place where wellness and wholeness and what we call "normality" are totally absent. As Kosmo says to Yahoodi near the end, "We're both infected with the same disease." If so, their shared victimization proves an antidote to loneliness.

Nor are the other proposed answers sufficient. Using the term "myth" in the traditional way, all of the possible optimistic solutions are found lacking—as a roll call of truisms indicates. Kosmo feels, early in the play, that he is getting "closer to the truth." By the end of the play, he can't hear the music anymore. Perhaps that is truth, but if so, it is not the longed-for respite he sought. Yahoodi thinks that if he were only famous and had money, he could "fly back to the city and put a needle" in his arm. Also, he states, "I could buy a farm in the country and raise a family and be a happy man" (154), expressing with dark humor two apparently incompatible wishes. And the illusion that fame and money are the equal of happiness is undermined by the experience of Marlene and Mae and Jesse James and Captain Kidd—and by Kosmo, who is "a famous pop star." Finally, the notion that love or art offers salvation is equally false, for although all of the characters claim they want a home and they all seem to want love, they carry within themselves the seeds of destruction of this type of stability. They wander and search, but they cannot escape themselves—as Yahoodi's sickly humorous desire for a needle in his arm, a farm in the country, and a family demonstrates. Nor is there a place such as that envisioned by Marlene: "Someplace where the sun always shines and the people dance. Someplace where there's music in the air" (192). A temptation to point to the end of the play where all of the characters join hands and dance and sing—like in the idyllic place seen by Marlene—will be contradicted by a reading of the words to the song "Home," and a recollection of the wanderings in the play, and of the characters who finally exit "out into the street." There is no final resting place. Perhaps Waco comes the closest to an accurate summation of the state in which the characters find themselves. They've traversed the globe, and Shepard unleashes them out into the world, literally. But as Waco admits: "I got nowheres to go and nothin' to see. Nowheres. And that's the truth" (176).

The impossibility of knowing anything definitive about oneself or one's acquaintances, or about the world, is obviously a message of *The Mad Dog Blues*, and a way Shepard has of saying that myth is not necessarily a traditional formula, but rather a sense of mystery, and perhaps a comic mystery at that. In *The Mad Dog Blues* Shepard's unusual treatment of real and fictitious celebrities leads either to hilarity or to a further sense of mystery, rather than to a convenient symbolic key.

One other especially effective comic play is *Forensic and the Navigators*. Although Shepard has been accused of being anti-feminist because his plays fail to cast a strong woman as a leading character, in a certain sense, his portrayal of women as objects to be used emphasizes that such an attitude is wrong. Although *Forensic and the Navigators* shows Oolan as abused by men, it does not follow that Shepard believes women should be abused by men. The character of Oolan was first played by Shepard's wife, and I believe the role indicates a respect for women—and at the same time offers an indictment of the way women are treated in our society. Despite these serious implications, though, much of the play is undeniably humorous.

As the play opens, Forensic and Emmet are sitting at a table smoking a pipe, plotting revolution, and wondering "where that woman is" with their breakfast. Oolan enters and circles the table flipping a pancake and catching it in a pan.

> Oolan: You boys should have told me what hour it was getting to be. Why, my goodness sakes, I look at the clock and the time is getting to be way past the time for you boys' breakfast. And you both know how uptight the two of you get when breakfast isn't just exactly when you get the most hungry. So here it is. Hot and ready.
> (She flips the pancake onto the table. Forensic and Emmet stare at the pancake as Oolan smiles. Emmet sits back in his chair. Oolan picks up the pipe and smokes it.)
> Emmet: How many times I gotta tell you I don't eat that buckwheat Aunt Jemima middle-class bullshit. I want Rice Krispies and nothing else. Is that clear?
> Forensic: Get that pancake off the conference table, you stupid girl. (56)

Oolan complies; she eats their pancake! There are several elements of humor in this scene. It is comic that two serious revolutionaries are treated like little boys, and it is hard to take them seriously when one of the most important issues in their lives is having their breakfast exactly on time. It is amusing that Oolan flips the pancake onto the very table which is the symbolic center of the revolution—a kind of comment on the importance of these men and their ideas. Finally, it is absurd that Emmet protests pancakes as too middle-class when the Rice Krispies he prefers are the epitome of conventional breakfast fare.

One source of humor in this play which was not discussed in the *The Unseen Hand* is Shepard's pointing out man's weak grasp of reality. The least alteration in what we have come to expect as basic (such as gravity, for example) throws us off guard: we are inflexible, unable to adapt. The way Shepard makes this point adds to the comedy, but the point itself is serious and, taken to its logical conclusion, furthers his basic view of man's situation as absurd. Oolan tries to tell the exterminators that they have the wrong house:

> 1st Exterminator: This is exactly the place, little girl.
> 2nd Exterminator: The table gives it away. Without the table or with the table in another place maybe it would be cause to call the home office. But with the table in the place it is and looking the way it does there is absolutely no doubt we have the right place. (58)

After this speech, Forensic and Emmet lift the table from underneath and move it, unseen by the exterminators, so that it looks as if the table moved itself. As a distraction, and a further note of humor and incongruity, Oolan sings "Ahab the Arab." When the exterminators realize that the table is in a different location, they are almost pathetic in the doubt cast on their former certainty; the very slight alteration is a threat to their world view. They cannot think for themselves because one small table has been moved a few feet. This is amusing, but also sad.

In the meantime Oolan has given serious thought as to how to solve a pressing problem for Emmet, one that's bothered him for years, a complaint that a few Rice Krispie pieces are lost as soon as milk is added to a full bowl. She suggests that he fill the bowl half full and then mush the Krispies down so that they can't overflow. The Krispies receive further attention when Emmet fears a threat from outside and he clutches the cereal box to his chest as if it were his most prized possession. He yells: "Hide the Krispies! Hide the Krispies! What'll we do?" (74). This farcical scene perhaps reaches its zenith when the 2nd Exterminator returns from an errand and exclaims: "Boy, is it ever weird out there" (75).

Yet the ending is serious; Michael Bloom has called it "apocryphal" (78). Smoke fills the stage and pours out to envelop the audience. It disappears very gradually, and when it is finally completely gone, the stage is bare.

Although I have concentrated on Shepard's witty verbal facility (and sometimes how that talent enters into the physical humor), it is worth noting that the physical comedy is often amusing in and of itself—as in *Fool for Love* when May and Eddie are hugging passionately—until she knees him in the groin. As with the verbal exchanges, the physical images are amusing because of the discrepancy between what we expect and what we are given. Shepard's finest moments come when he actively grafts the audience's imagination onto his imaginative world so that it feels and thinks finely and in tune with his characters; but since he never wholly sustains a vision throughout any play, the audience experiences personally the conviction that the world in which it has an intellectual and emotional stake lacks coherence. That Shepard succeeds in getting his audiences to invest in the microcosm he crafts, whether that microcosm is serious or amusing, safe or menacing (or all of the above), attests that the playwright is in command of the art he produces and that his visions are more powerful than our ability or desire to resist them. The touches of humor and mystery he incorporates go far in making us want to enter into the spirit of "play" which enticed Shepard to the theater.

References

Bloom, Michael. "Visions of the End: The Early Plays." *American Dreams: The Imagination of Sam Shepard.* Ed. Bonnie Marranca. New York: Performing Arts Journal Publication, 1981.

Chubb, Kenneth, and the editors of *Theatre Quarterly.* "Metaphors, Mad Dogs, and Old Time Cowboys," *Theatre Quarterly* (1974): 16.

Marranca, Bonnie, ed. *American Avenues: The Imagination of Sam Shepard.* New York: Performing Arts Journal Publications, 1981.

Shepard, Sam. "Forensic and the Navigators." *The Unseen Hand and Other Plays.* New York: Urizen Books, 1972.

————. "Language, Visualization, and the Inner Library," *The Drama Review* (Dec. 1977).

————. "La Turista," *Sam Shepard: Seven Plays.* Introduction by Richard Gilman. New York: Bantam, 1981.

————. "The Mad Dog Blues" in *Angel City, Curse of the Starving Class and Other Plays.* Vancouver: Talonbooks, n.d.

————. "The Unseen Hand." *The Unseen Hand and Other Plays.* New York: Urizen Books, 1972.

WHO WAS ICARUS'S MOTHER?
THE POWERLESS MOTHER FIGURES
IN THE PLAYS OF SAM SHEPARD

Doris Auerbach

The father of Icarus was Daedalus, best known as the architect of the Minoan labyrinth, an Athenian distinguished for his ingenuity and cunning. He was later imprisoned in the very labyrinth that he designed, where he invented two pairs of wings which enabled him and his son to escape. The son did not heed the father's warning and flew too high, burnt his wings and plunged into the sea. We know little of Icarus' mother, Naucrate, except that she was a slave at the Minoan court. She apparently was as unimportant to the myth as she is in Shepard's play, *Icarus's Mother*, as no such character appears in it. She is thus an apt personification of the dominated, powerless mother figures in Sam Shepard's plays.

From the mother, lying ill in bed in *Rock Garden*, one of his earliest plays, to the two flaky mothers in *A Lie of the Mind*, his latest, Sam Shepard has created a series of mother figures who are too weak to counteract the violence of the fathers. They lack the will and the power to restore order in their world, to bring about a family in balance, one that can nurture its children.

Shepard has used as his paradigm for the family in crisis, the overwhelming cultural myth of the American West. He portrays an eternal battle between the women gatherers who settle down, grow food and create civilization, and men, the nomadic hunters, who survive by violence and flee the ties of family and commitment. His protagonists are:

> Men on the run, harried into the forest, and out to sea, down the river and into combat—anywhere to avoid 'civilization,' which is to say, the confrontation of a man and a woman. (Fiedler xx)

Baylor, the brutal father, in *A Lie of the Mind*, seems to speak for all of Shepard's fathers:

> I could be up in the wild country huntin' antelope. I could be raising a string of pack-mules up in there. Doin' somethin' useful. But no, I gotta play nursemaid to a bunch a' feeble-minded women down there in civilization who can't take care of themselves. I gotta waste my days away makin' sure they eat and have a roof over their heads. . . . (*Lie* 107)

Fathers in Shepard's plays escape the ties of families and civilization into the desert and the Western wilderness with its promised dream of freedom. They leave wives and children in the elusive search for themselves. As Meg, one of the mothers in *A Lie of the Mind*, mockingly says: "If only your life was free of females, then y'd be free yourself" (*Lie* 107). But the elusive fathers who escape women and family never find their dreams. They become like the unseen father in *True West*, a drunken bum who lives alone in the desert. The cowboy figure in Shepard's plays has run out of room to run. Unlike Lorraine's father in *Lie* who "started a town on a mesquite stump. He just hung his hat on it and a whole town sprang up" (*Lie* 67), today's cowboy faces a new West, one made up of rusty cars, shopping centers and freeways. The family that Shepard portrays over and over again is one that cannot nurture its children, that has become as fruitless and sterile as the betrayed American dream of the West. At its core is the violence of the fathers, the brutal and cold world of the archetypal power struggle of son against father, of brother against brother. The feminine principle is powerless to intercede and stop the endless progression from one violent man to another. Vince, the questing motherless protagonist of *Buried Child*, becomes aware of carrying on this tradition, personified in the play by Dodge, the grandfather:

> I could see myself in the windshield. My face. My eyes. I studied
> everything about it. As though I was looking at another man. As
> though I could see his whole face behind him. Like a mummy's face. I
> saw him dead and alive at the same time. In the same breath. . . . And
> then his face changed. His face became his father's face. And it went
> on like that. Changing. Clear on back to faces I'd never seen before
> but still recognized. . . . (*Buried Child* 70).

The sons are unable to end the repetition of abandonment. They're
doomed to repeat the obsessive behavior of the fathers, rootless
wanderers in search of a home. The folded American flag and the box
containing the ashes of the drunken father who abandoned the family in
Lie become concrete symbols of the impossibility of love, of
communion between abandoned son and rejecting father. How close
Shepard feels to the deserted sons in his plays can be seen in his
reminiscence of the death of his own father: "I had my father cremated,
you know. There wasn't much left of him to begin with. They give
you this box with ashes in it" (Putzel 158). Like the father-figures in
his plays, Shepard's father was a tyrannical, heavy-drinking, ex-army
officer who left his family. The fruitless attempt of the son to reach the
father figure is shown at the end of the first act of *Lie*. Jake opens the
box of his father's ashes, "Blows lightly into it, sending a soft puff of
ashes into the beam of the spotlight. Spotlight slowly fades to black"
(*Lie* 58).

Shepard began the exploration of the decline and fall of the
American dream, with the family as a metaphor, in *Curse of the
Starving Class* (1976). He describes a crumbling family that is no
longer viable. It cannot withstand the destructive forces crushing it from
without and the disintegration from within. The father is an
irresponsible drunk and the mother is a woman who has survived by
withdrawing. The children are left feeling cheated and stunted by the
ultimate starvation—lack of love. The "curse" of the title "refers to the
inevitability of generation after generation repeating the same
meaningless act. The curse of the father is passed on to the son"
(Auerbach 49). As Weston, the father, says: "I never saw my old man's
poison until I was much older than you. Much older. And then you
know how I recognized it?—Because I saw myself infected with it"
(*Curse* 49).

The "curse" also refers to menstruation, which Ella, the mother,
comments upon at length in the play. If the poison Weston refers to is

transmitted from father to son, then the "curse" is transmitted from mother to daughter. But without removing the label of curse from a woman's biological functions and changing the compulsive violence of the male, a more fertile environment in which children can develop is impossible. Weston understands that family was founded on flesh and blood: ". . . family wasn't just a social thing. It was an animal thing. It was a reason of nature that we're altogether under the same roof" (*Curse* 104). But Weston upsets the balance of nature and the family, because to him the eagle's ingestion of the lambs' testes represents only masculine power and dominance. In his long speech describing the castration of lambs, he expresses his feelings when the giant eagle swoops down for "those fresh little remnants of manlihood . . ." (*Curse* 102):

> Somethin' brought me straight up off the ground and I started yelling my fool head off. Cheerin' for that eagle. I never felt like that since the first day I went up in a B-49. . . . And every time I cut a lamb I'd throw those balls up on top a' the shed roof. And every time he'd come down like the Cannonball Express on that roof and every time I got that feeling. (*Curse* 102)

The female's fertility, however, is seen merely as a curse.

In his epitaph on the American family as an institution and the decay of the American dream, *Buried Child* (1978), Shepard exposes the skeleton in the American family closet—the theme of incest which reemerges in all his major plays to follow. Shepard has always been noted for his skillful use of archetypal myths. As early as 1969 in *The Holy Ghostly* he introduced the eternal struggle between father and son. There is no mention of a mother figure in that early play, only the cowboy son returning home to confront the father and wrest power from him. In Shepard's depiction of the American West, the cowboy is the violent, isolated victor who flees from civilization and defeats the attempts of the mother to create a nurturing family. In *Buried Child*, however, Shepard reveals the struggle of the father to keep his son from gaining power. As I have noted elsewhere, Dodge, the father who has always 'dodged' responsibility for his sons, is a threatening father whose infanticidal impulse still haunts him and creates unconscious guilt in the audience. The powerless mother figure is not only unable to protect her children but has the violence of the father projected onto her: "You never saw a bitch eating her puppies?" (*Buried Child* 54). Like

Weston in *Curse*, Dodge sees paternity only as a phallic exercise of potency. He rejects caring for his children, for, like Cronus, he fears death at the hands of his progeny.

The farm, like the family, has grown barren; only Tilden, the profoundly burnt-out son, believes the fertile paradise he vaguely remembers can be restored again. Tilden is one of the defenseless males who is aligned with the equally powerless mothers against the fathers' world of power, dominance and violence. Tilden, the tiller of the soil, wanted to create the son who would make the land fruitful again, the son who would be strong enough to turn his back on the world of the fathers, who would create a new world which would end patriarchy's violent hegemony. This was the child he conceived with his mother, Halie, who like Eve, bore the child in pain, the child that "begged" to be born (Auerbach 60). This was the child that Tilden nurtured: "he'd walk all night out in the pasture with it. Talkin' to it. Singing to it. Used to hear him singing to it" (*Buried Child* 65). This was the child that threatened Dodge's patriarchal power and was killed by him. The mother and the nurturing procreator, Tilden, were unable to protect it. Dodge commits infanticide: "Couldn't allow a thing like that to grow up in the middle of our lives" (*Buried Child* 61). The existence of this child, conceived through incest, would destroy the violent world of the father. But how else are new worlds founded?—With whom did Adam's son mate but with Eve? The play ends like a miracle play with the symbol of the resurrection. The child is taken from the tomb, tended by Tilden and carried up, not to the patriarchal figure who lies dead on stage before us but to the mother who is waiting above. The struggle of father against son is only one of Shepard's mythical themes. The other archetypical situation he portrays is the ancient conflict of brother against brother. As early as 1967, he introduces the rivalry between two brothers in *Melodrama Play*, as the means of exploring the lust for power and its connection to the creative drive. In *True West* (1980) the spiritual death of the American family is again related to the disappearance of the western wilderness and its promise of freedom. The father's mythical western world of manliness, rootlessness and violence is pitted against the world of mom and her kitchen. Shepard raises the question of what is the true west. Is it the world of the cowboy who faces life alone with his horse? The lone John Wayne who survives without the woman, family, home or love, an anarchic figure alienated from society? Is it the west eulogized in *Geography of a Horse Dreamer*?

> Yes! I remember that! I remember thinking this is the West! This is really the West! Then we got to that town where Buffalo Bill lived. . . . Oh what a town! . . . And at night. At night it was magical. Like praying. I'd never heard such a silence as that. Nowhere on the earth . . . So vast and lonely. Just the brisk cold night blowing in through the hotel window. And outside, the blue peaks of the Big Horn mountains. The moon shining on their snowy caps. The prairie stretching out and out like a great ocean. I felt that God was in me then. The earth held me in his arms. (*Geography* 142)

Or it is the west he recalls in the preface to *Unseen Hand* (1969)?

> Azusa is a real place. A real town. About 40 miles outside of Los Angeles. Just off the San Bernardino Freeway. Its real slogan is 'everything from A to Z in the USA.' And it's just like that, a collection of junk. Mostly people. It's the neighboring town of Duarte where I grew up. These towns are obsessions of mine because of their accidentalness. . . . They grew out of nothing or nowhere. Originally the valley was covered with citrus groves. . . . Eventually Los Angeles had a population kick back. People who couldn't make it in the big city just drove away from it. They got so far and just quit the road. . . . Lots of them lived in trailer camps. . . . It was a temporary society that became permanent. (*Unseen Hand* 20)

Shepard's conflicting depictions of the west share an aloneness, a lack of human commitment. The two brothers, who ostensibly represent the opposing world of father and mother, each long for the sphere that is denied him. The violent brutish Lee, whose identification with the father is obvious, who has been living alone in the desert with a pitbull, admits at one point that he longs for mom's suburban paradise. The intellectual, controlled Austin who belongs to mom's neat little world, longs to become like the Old Man. The structural device for the struggle between the brothers is the writing of a screenplay depicting the true west. Lee, the anarchic adventurer, has the vision while Austin, the self-disciplined professional, has the technique. The Nietzschean Apollinian/Dionysian antithesis is demonstrated on stage. Neither the screenplay nor a coherent conception of America can be created. The worlds of the father and the mother can never be reconciled. The Old Man may be a drunken bum, but his influence overwhelms the stage with its power, while Mom, whose kitchen is in ruins at the end, retreats in defeat. In a powerful scene the brothers stand amid the debris of the kitchen surrounded by toasters, endlessly popping toast. Austin, who has been begging Lee to permit him to return to the desert with him, humbly offers the brutish brother a plate of buttered toast which he smashes. Austin drops to his knees and picks up the toast, in a gesture William Kleb calls, "A mortification ritual, a final submission to Lee's authority," (Kleb 19) an apt metaphor for the defeat of the world of the mother at the hands of the violent male.

Mom appears in the play in the last scene, a dazed, remote figure who, like Ella in *Curse*, has only survived by emotionally withdrawing from the field of battle. She looks around the battle field—her ruined kitchen, her dead plants—as powerless to intercede between the warring brothers as she has been to mediate between father and son. She no longer has the will to act; like a zombie, she leaves the stage to check into a hotel, oblivious to the brothers rolling on the floor in mortal combat. The play ends with the image of the two clashing eternally on a darkling plain.

In one of Shepard's commercially most successful creations, both on stage and on film, *Fool for Love* (1985), the themes of sibling rivalry, incest, domineering fathers and weak mothers are intertwined into a powerful assault on the audience. The stage direction reads, "The play is to be performed relentlessly without a break" (*Fool* 113), and the two lovers alternately maul and paw each other with a violence seldom seen on stage. The rejecting father figure appears on stage in the form of an old stumblebum who "exists only in the minds of May and Eddie, even though they might talk to him directly and acknowledge his physical presence" (*Fool* 15).

Eddie is both the son who has been abandoned and the husband who abandoned, unable to rid himself of his obsession with the father and his compulsive sadomasochistic tie to May, who is both abandoned child and wife. The verbal and physical battles in the claustrophobic motel room are a continuation of the fight between the brothers in *True West*, for May and Eddie are not only lovers but siblings as well. Just as May has continued the incestuous relationship for fifteen years, their mothers, the Old Man's wives, compulsively clung to him. They were not only powerless but unwilling to fight for their children, two more of Shepard's macho-fantasy women who become obsessed, become fools for love. The incestuous lovers who have been, as the Old Man says, marked by their mothers, "who put their stamps on you" (*Fool* 49), have been made incompetent to survive in the world of the father. No matter how violently they attack each other, they can't break loose from the primitive blood ties which fetter them to each other. Eddie dreams vainly of building ". . . a little pipe corral to keep the horses. Have a big vegetable garden. Some chickens maybe" (*Fool* 23). But their love is doomed to infertility; the American dream, the American family, can't be revitalized by their ambivalent sibling relationship. Although May seems to be an active agent in the play, in effect she plays a schizophrenic role—the fool for love, always waiting for the man who abandons her, as well as the warring brother figure—a veritable Abel in drag.

Shepard's latest and perhaps definitive statement on the state of the American family is the expansive *A Lie of the Mind*. Self-referentially, the playwright has taken the title from his comic operetta, *The Sad Lament of Pecos Bill on the Eve of Killing His Wife* (1976). The hapless heroine, Slue-foot Sue, sings to console the husband who has killed her: "Your crime was invented by lies of the mind. It's a crime when a lie is so true." To which Bill replies, "But I was fathered by liars and my offspring was too. Oh how can I ever escape it . . ." (*Sad Lament* 96).

How indeed can Shepard's America, peopled by violent men, survive? How can these men "escape" the repetition of the sins of the fathers against women in brutal emotionless marriages? Are the lies the ever-receding dream of a nurturing family, of a viable, fruitful land? Are they the blood ties? Surely Shepard has never given a more pessimistic diagnosis of the state of the American dream. The frontier has run out; the west is no longer big enough for every loner to start his own town. It has turned into a bloody field where the abandoned son has turned to patricide, and obsessive love has led to attempted murder. Jake, the tormented protagonist, goes to avenge the abandoned family, goes in search of the father and challenges him to a lethal drinking bout.

> They start right off with double shots of tequila and lime. At first it was like the brotherhood they'd just remembered. But then it started to shift. After about the fourth double shot it started to go in a whole different direction. . . . There was a meanness that started to come out of both of them like these hidden snakes. A terrible meanness that was like—murder almost. It was murder. . . . Jake

came up with a brilliant idea. He said, since we were only about a
mile from the American border we should hit every bar and continue
the race until we got to the other side. First one then the other side
won. . . . Right then I knew what Jake had in mind. Jake had decided
to kill him. . . . He knew, knew what was gonna happen. Dad
couldn't even walk any more. . . . He was trying to beat his own son
to the border. He didn't even know what country he was in any more!
Jake murdered him. (*Lie* 92)

The women are too ineffectual to intercede successfully. As Sally,
the sister, says, "Dad wouldn't let me near him. I couldn't get near him.
. . . he wouldn't let me help him" (*Lie* 94).

Jake was unsuccessful in reaching his father, in creating a
communion between father and son in a loveless environment. He was
equally unsuccessful in creating love out of tortured lust that sought
only to dominate and control the beloved. The obsession turns to
violence and death. Jake is a time bomb suspended between the
unreachable father and the woman he obsessively wants to possess.

Shepard doubles the stakes in *Lie*, putting on a split stage two
families in extremis; two rejecting brutal fathers; two ineffectual
mothers; two brothers, one tormenting, the other assuaging; connected
by the two lovers—Jake, the wife beater, and Beth, the battered, brain-
injured wife.

In none of his other plays has Shepard shown more strongly the
impossibility of a healthy family life or a successful relationship
between lovers. As Clive Barnes has noted, "Men live for hunting and
dominating women, the women live until they die" (*NYTCR* 108). The
play presents us with two dotty mother figures, each reinforcing the
picture of the powerlessness of dominated women. Lorraine, Jake's
dippy mother, has transferred her devotion from the father who deserted
her to the oldest son. There is no love left in her for Frankie, the
"good" son, or Sally, the daughter. When Jake leaves to find the wife he
had almost beaten to death, Lorraine takes it as another manifestation of
abandonment: "Is there any good reason for that? You tell me. Isn't
there enough to suffer already? We got all kinda good reasons to suffer
without men cooking up more" (*Lie* 84).

His departure makes her feel helpless to protect the son. "He's run
off to the wild world when he could've stayed here under my protection.
He could've stayed here for ever and no one could've touched him" (*Lie*
87). She's equally impotent to free herself of the father who had walked

out on her: ". . . He still alive in me. You understand that? He still walkin' around inside me" (*Lie* 91).

Meg, Beth's mother, has been completely worn down by the emotional brutality of her husband, Baylor. As she kneels, rubbing mink oil into his feet, she vainly tries to make him understand the quintessential difference between powerless women and aggressive males:

MEG: The female—the female one needs—the other.
BAYLOR: What other?
MEG: The male. The male one.
BAYLOR: Oh.
MEG: But the male one—doesn't really need the other. Not the same way.
BAYLOR: I don't get ya.
MEG: The male one goes off by himself. Leaves. He needs something else. But he doesn't know what it is. He doesn't really know what he needs. So he ends up dead. By himself. (*Lie* 105)

Beth, the wife, whom Jake in a frustrated, jealous rage has beaten almost to death, is the brain-injured victim of not only her husband but her rejecting father as well: "This—this is my father. He's given up love. Love is dead for him. My mother is dead for him. Things live for him to be killed. Only death counts for him" (*Lie* 51).

Like Lorraine, whose phantom husband is still alive in her, like Meg, who cherishes the first kiss Baylor has given her in 20 years, Beth cannot rid herself of Jake. Aphasic from the brain injury caused by his attack, she struggles to explain:

BETH: NAAH! you gan' stop my head. Nobody! Nobody stop my head. My head is me. Heez in me. You gan stop him in me. Nobody gan stop him in me.
MIKE: This guy tried to kill you! How can you still want a man who tried to kill you? He's the one who did this to you!
BETH: Heez MY HaaaaaaaaaaaaaaaaaaRT. (*Lie* 17)

Women and men are locked in an eternal power struggle in which the women are always subjugated. Not only the women, but those men who have not repressed the need for human contact and feelings are defeated in Shepard's bleak vision. His plays show the inability to survive of such men as Hoss in *Tooth of Crime*, Austin in *True West*, Tilden in *Buried Child* and Frankie in *Lie*. Like the women who reinforce the myth of women's preference for abusive men, the "good" brothers long to emulate the ones who have bonded with the world of the fathers. The pathetic Beth seeks to integrate the two conflicting male personalities into one ideal lover:

> "You have the same voice. Maybe you could be him. Pretend. Maybe. Just him. Just like him. But soft. With me. Gentle. Like a woman-man. . . . You could be better. Better man. Maybe. Without hate. You could be my sweet man. You could. Pretend to be. Try. My sweetest man." (*Lie* 16)

But Frankie, like the mother figures, is too weak to oppose the aggressive males. He accepts their right to dominate. This is shown in *Lie* by the antlers of the killed deer. All Baylor wants is the rack, the symbol of the male. The bareness of this is emphasized in the play by Baylor's refusal to eat the deer's meat. He's interested only in the kill. The deer carcass joins the toast in *True West*, the carrots in *Buried Child* and the artichokes in *Curse* as metaphors for the American family that can no longer feed its children, for the land that can no longer sustain the dream.

Jake is vanquished in *Lie* by Mike, Beth's equally violent brother. Shepard has always insisted on the peculiarly American wellsprings of his inspiration. Yet despite his self-created myth of the western loner, his works have often paid homage to European poets and playwrights who have touched the nerve in Shepard's imagination. References to the French poets Nerval, Villon and Baudelaire abound in *Cowboy Mouth*; The title of *Tooth of Crime* is drawn from a poem by another French poet, Mallarmé; and the similarity in theme to Brecht's *Jungle of Cities* is striking. In *Lie*, Shepard evokes the work of another European playwright. At the end of the play, the vanquished Jake appears on stage: "Walking on his knees straight toward the audience with the American flag between his teeth and stretched taut on either side of his head like a set of driving reins for a draft horse. Behind Jake, holding an end of the flag in each hand, Mike walks along, clucking to Jake like a horse and tugging the reins now and then" (*Lie* 120). The image evokes Pozzo and Lucky, in Beckett's *Waiting for Godot*, the picture of humanity locked in a battle of eternal dominance and submission. The now powerless, emasculated Jake, in an attempt at expiation, wills Beth to Frankie: "You stay with him" (*Lie* 129). Frankie, who is as linked to the dominant brother as the mothers are to the dominant fathers, rejects the responsibility: "Jake!! Jake, you gotta take her with you!! It's not true Jake! She belongs to you!" (*Lie* 123) But the brain-injured Beth clings to the "woman-man" Frankie, whose leg injury seems to be gangrenous and who is threatened with amputation of his leg.

Just as longing for a healthy family is proscribed by the breaking of incest tabu in *Buried Child* and *Fool for Love*, so its possibility is denied in *A Lie of the Mind*. Beth and Frankie are victims of the violence of their father and the helplessness of their mothers to protect them. The image of the powerless lovers as a foundation for a new fruitful land and nurturing family mocks the dream's realization.

References

Fiedler, Leslie. *Love and Death in the American Novel*. Meridian Books, 1960.

Kleb, William. "Worse Than Being Homeless: *True West* and the Divided Self" in *American Dreams, The Imagination of Sam Shepard*. Performing Arts Journal Publications, 1981.

New York Theatre Critics Reviews (1985).

Putzel, Steve. "Audience Complicity in the Plays of Shepard," *Modern Drama*, 3.2 (1980).

Shepard, Sam. "Azusa Is a Real Place: Sam Shepard Writes a Special Preface to '*The Unseen Hand*,'" *Plays and Players*, 20 (1973).

———. *Buried Child*. Uriza Books, 1979.

———. *Curse of the Starving Class*. Urizen Books, 1976.

———. *Fool for Love*. City Lights Books, 1979.

———. *Geography of a Horse Dreamer*. Grove, 1974.

———. *A Lie of the Mind*. New American Library, 1986.

———. *The Sad Lament of Pecos Bill on the Eve of Killing His Wife*. City Lights Books, 1979.

STORY ITSELF

Christopher Brookhouse

Beginning with *The Curse of the Starving Class*, a core of similar characters, interiors, implied landscapes, visual motifs, symbols, themes, and structural devices occur and recur in various combinations in each of Shepard's plays. One play seems to emerge from another; the works are almost a single play, each with a different emphasis and set of variations, that emphasize the idea of storytelling. The plays evolve through repeated situations and structures exploring the relationships of character's story and audience's story and author's story.

Shepard's characters are storytellers. In *Curse*, for example, long narrative monologues stand out. Weston, particularly, has two lengthy speeches, both early in Act III: one introducing the cat/eagle story, which will serve as a concluding comment on the whole play, and the other detailing his rebirth, his return to sobriety and responsibility. Both speeches are important but neither gives quite the nod to the future course of Shepard's work as does Wesley's monologue in Act I or Emma's at the beginning of Act II.

In the first act, Emma begins to tell her plan, her fantasy of escape into her future. "I was going to head for Baja California," she tells her mother. "I was going to work on fishing boats," she goes on, concluding with her plans to be a writer, a storyteller. "Just like that guy," she says, referring to B. Traven.

Emma is a storyteller in a significantly different way from Weston. Weston recounts what has taken place, Emma is imagining what will take place. In the second act Emma eagerly enlarges her fantasy to include the relationship of Ella and Taylor. In Emma's mind, and through her words to us, she describes Ella and Taylor driving in Mexico, experiencing car trouble, and encountering Emma the mechanic, whom they don't recognize but trust, to their loss of car parts and money, before being set on their way again.

Emma's story is about the future; Weston's is about the past, as is Wesley's at the onset of the play. Wesley describes the events of the previous evening which result in the condition of the house when the play opens. Wesley's words establish the past but do so with a particular emphasis on his own perceptions. His account begins with pastoral unity and progress through fear to the memories of his father's drunken return. The themes and images from Wesley's memory present themes and images that will occur throughout the play just as Weston's stories of the past refer to images and themes that become reference points during the play. However, there is a difference. At the end of Wesley's monologue a sudden shift in the grammatical form of the memory takes place, a shift away from first person and the use of present participles. "Then far off the freeway could be heard," Wesley says. The passive construction calls special attention to itself first because the syntax signals a story coming to an end, as if in telling the story the storyteller is at last no longer there in first person as he has been throughout the rest of the account, and second because the teller is displaced by the things of the landscape that surrounds the story.

In the larger context of Shepard's work, Emma's speech and Wesley's point to a self-consciousness about storytelling which foregrounds the form or the idea of storytelling instead of emphasizing the content of stories. Such self-consciousness, on the part of character as well as author, will cause the audience to become aware of the relationship between the form of storytelling and the truth or invention of the content of the story that is being told. In *Curse*, however, such awareness is just beginning. In no speech is there a reason to distrust or question what is told. What Wesley says is probably true, as is what Weston says later on. Emma's story may raise the question of possibility (could what she fantasizes happen?), but as a fantasy of future revenge her story reveals her mind through the images that she uses. What will happen, though, if the stories Shepard's characters tell start off sounding like truth, but then draw the listener in one direction and abandon him. What will happen when Shepard arrives at the notion that the fantasy may do more than create the future; the fantasy may also create the past?

How we respond to words is at least in part the result of what we think the words are intended to signify. In *Buried Child* the words seem to start off telling us a realistic story about a family we recognize. We seem to find a familiar pattern of aging, decay, and rural misery. We think we know these people. We have heard stories about them before. We probably agree with Dodge that Tilden has stolen the corn. We probably accept Halie's remarks about a successful day at the races even if time has blurred her ability to recall where the race was run. However when Halie launches into her account of Ansel, we have reason to doubt her. Her version of Ansel's history is so full of cultural mythology it sounds unreal. Ansel, Halie insists, was both athlete and soldier. He was destroyed by the Mob and Catholics. "Catholic women are the Devil incarnate." Perhaps Halie is just full of prejudices. After she leaves the house, Dodge begins his memory about baseball, but the facts don't work. Dodge couldn't have been a young man when Stan Musial was playing in the major leagues. What is the audience supposed to believe? The audience and Shelly are more or less in the same position. She enters with her outsider's point of view influenced by other cultural forms of storytelling. Observing the house, she says, "It's like a Norman Rockwell cover or something." Shelly's entrance in Act II is like entering the play all over again. We know what is inside the house isn't a Norman Rockwell family but we don't know much more. "She thinks she's going to uncover the truth of the matter. Like a detective or something," Dodge says.

The audience too is a detective of sorts, trying to make sense of things. But to make sense of things, we fall back on our own stories, our own versions of things, or at least the versions we expect to take place. *Buried Child* is, among other things, a play about the difference in stories, ours and Shepard's. We are led into the play with certain expectations. Tilden probably stole the corn. It's logical at first to believe he did. Gradually we learn he didn't, which means the story we believed we were going to hear when we began the play won't help us when we confront possibilities and events that are not played out in the logical patterns of realism but exist instead on the plains of myth and psychic mythology that subvert the assumption of realism's logic and order.[1]

Buried Child established Shepard's concern with the heart of drama, that interaction of writer, player, and audience, each telling stories at the same time; the audience approaches the play with the stories it wants to believe and finds comfortable to believe, and meets the author telling another story.

The slow drawing out of various versions of a past event in *Buried Child* will eventually be paralleled by the structure of *Fool for Love*, while the foremost structural device of *Curse*, reversal (of both material, spiritual, and physical conditions) links *Curse* closely to *True West*. However the two later plays repeat structures of the earlier works with more economy; that is, both *Curse* and *Buried Child* are, each, almost two plays. In *Curse* the comic attempts of Ella and Weston to sell property, each reversing the other, and to deal with the threat of retaliation for Weston's debts, are often uneasily combined with the themes of the nature of the family, the hopelessness of the future, and the ritual rebirth of Weston and the reversal of Wesley's nurturing and responsible attitudes. The various reversals in *True West* are more controlled and create a stronger unity. In *Buried Child* the focus on Vince's return and his inheritance of Dodge's position (position physically as a sign of spiritual position is another device Shepard is fond of using), is at times hard to balance with the possibilities of hope suggested by the unburying of the child and Halie's final affirmation of a miracle and the power of the sun (son). Of course, my comments betray my own prejudices and in turn my own story.

In any event, *True West* is clearly about storytelling, overtly so when Lee verbally seduces Saul into a golf match which results in Saul's commitment to Lee's story of the West. Lee, who may talk a good game about being self-reliant and anti-establishment, but who is sold on the culture's approval of blondes, Mexican tile, and copperware, builds a story that comments on his relationship with Austin; the pursuer and the pursued are both ignorant of their destinations. Austin criticizes Lee's characters for being illusions of character, "Fantasies of a long lost boyhood." The point of Austin's criticism is truth. Lee's story seems to lack truth, to lack reality. Austin recounts the episode of how their father lost his teeth and his false teeth as well. "Now that's a real story. True to life," Austin says.

The title of Shepard's play refers to the question of truth, and Austin as well tries to convince Saul that he, Austin, is more qualified to write the truth. "I swallow the smog. I watch the news in color. I shop in the Safeway. I'm the one who's in touch." It turns out, however, that Austin retreats from his urban vision and returns to his imagination and his fantasies about living on the desert. Like so much of the play, Austin's change seems one more reversal, one more changing places with Lee. Lee wants to change place with Austin. Lee wants to settle down on a ranch. Their reversal of positions suggests their oneness (as it does in the situations of Wesley and Weston). Even Saul "thinks we're the same person," Lee says; later their mother underscores this when she suggests that despite going their separate ways, Lee and Austin, their father too, will "probably wind up on the same desert sooner or later."

Both Lee and Austin want to tell stories, but they can't do it without each other, which again suggests their oneness. Their vision of reality is split; there is no center of meaning, no outward reality, no focus of truth and reality that sustains their stories. There are only other stories, old stories. Austin finally turns against his story. He could write it, but he won't. He chooses the desert. Lee has less choice. He can't put his own story down on paper without help. The one successful storyteller, in an extended sense, is Picasso. The mother's confusion over Picasso's appearance at the local museum comes about because she fails to understand the artist and his art are one—where the art goes there also goes the artist. For Lee and Austin their failure at storytelling becomes their lives as well. The failed artist and the failed, or absent art, are also one. In this context, *True West* may be a cautionary and reflexive work, one in which its author is staring inward. This play, which audiences seem to find more accessible than *Curse* or *Buried Child*, is, perhaps, less complex than those plays. Does the play signal a point when its author falls back upon a refinement of the skills and material he has learned and has presented in earlier works? Does the failure of Austin and Lee hint at a self-awareness on Shepard's part, a concern for his own storytelling? Is he too aware of his 'old' stories?

If *True West* is about getting a story told, *Fool for Love* is about revision, and the separate versions of the past. That past is less opaque than the past events in *Buried Child*; they are drawn out in response in part to the presence of a stranger, but again the past is explained, or revised, to a stranger. Shelly becomes Martin. Because the story in

Fool is less saturated with myth than the events in *Buried Child*, the audience perhaps has less to ask about. The storytellers agree on certain parts of each other's story. The differences, however, are significant and are cues to the limitation of each teller and the ways in which the play explores the sense that the storyteller is a victim of his own story. Neither Eddie nor May is entirely capable of understanding how his or her story has been influenced by perceptions of their parents.

May, whose early actions in the play mirror the desperation of her mother's actions angrily refers to the way Eddie uses her. First she says, "you're either gonna' erase me or have me erased," a confirmation of the bond between imagination and the composition. Then she reacts angrily to Eddie's pastoral dream of settling in Wyoming. "You keep comin' up here with this lame country dream life with chickens and vegetables and I can't stand any of it." She continues, "How many times have you done this to me? . . . Suckered me into some dumb little fantasy. . . ." Eddie replies, "It's not fantasy." May's response is what Shepard has been telling us for a long time. "It's all a fantasy," she says.

The Old Man complicates the discussion. After The Old Man starts off his comments to Eddie by saying, "I thought you were supposed to be a fantasist, right? . . . You dream things up."—The Old Man points out the picture on the wall of Barbara Mandrell which doesn't exist ("There is no picture") but the audience is drawn into agreeing with Eddie, who "stares at the wall," picturing in his mind what The Old Man's mind has already put there. We agree to see the picture. Here again, Shepard is drawing the audience into cooperating with the characters and with himself in creating the story.

The Old Man asks Eddie if he could believe The Old Man is married to Barbara Mandrell. Eddie says no. "That's realism," The Old Man answers, meaning Eddie's answer refers to a verifiable reality, one where a marriage certificate would prove the point, that realm of the verifiable and logical that Shepard forces us to abandon in a play like *Buried Child*.

"I'm actually married to Barbara Mandrell in my mind," The Old Man responds. Then he asks a question of Eddie, but the question is one the audience must answer as well. "Can you understand that?" "Sure," Eddie says. The answer affirms the bond between character, storytellers, and audience.

May herself is also concerned with pictures, specifically her mind's invented pictures of the countess, Eddie's mysterious lover. The Old Man is settled with his picture; May is unsettled with hers. "All I see is a picture of you. You and her. I don't even know if the picture's real anymore. I don't even care. It's a made up picture. It invades my head." The fantasy is more painful than the actual events: "And this picture stings me even more than if I'd actually seen you with her," May says.

Eddie tries to comfort May. "We'll always be connected," he says. She replies, "You made all that up," referring to his own story of the past. "Nothing happened! Nothing ever happened!" May's protest echoes Bradley's to Shelly. "Nothing's wrong here! Nothing's ever been wrong!"

The version of the past that Eddie tells Martin contains mostly romantic details of The Old Man's walk through the the night, details of communion between father and son such as the shared whiskey, ending with a vision of undying love when Eddie and May first see each other. May's version stresses her mother's suffering and obsession: "She knew she was crossing this forbidden zone but she couldn't help herself." May's mother finds The Old Man and he disappears. May's mother tries to separate May and Eddie. Eddie's mother kills herself. "Eddie's mother blew her brains out. Didn't she, Eddie?"

The Old Man protests. "That's the dumbest version I ever heard in my whole life. She never blew her brains out." The Old Man wants Eddie to refute May's story. The appeal is less to fact than to gender. "I wanna' hear the male side a' this thing. You gotta' represent me now."

Eddie confirms that his mother killed herself. "It was your gun," he tells The Old Man, who then begins his own story to the extent that he refers his actions to his love for May's mother. "She kept opening up her heart to me," he says.

The stories agree on several details, but finally but we are left with omissions and gaps. Again, Shepard, who isn't careless or bored to the point of omitting details, is telling us a story with clues, leading us on by them as if clues fill out a reasonable and complete explanation: who did what to whom and when. Yet the story is more than details or facts; it is perspective, a storyteller's relationship to facts. And more again— storytelling involves gender; because gender arranges perspective. The storyteller's story is always his own story, but also part of a whole that can never, perhaps, be put together again. As Lee and Austin seem one, or as Saul sees them that way, May and Eddie are one: "We got sick at night when we were apart." So, too, the Old Man and May's mother were one: "We were completely whole." The force, though, of Shepard's plays is generally centrifugal. The whole comes apart. Eddie leaves and May packs her suitcase to continue on her own journey until she meets Eddie once again.

The Old Man ends the play speaking to the audience. Only Martin is present and cannot see The Old Man, so The Old Man addresses us. He affirms the power of the imagination, the power of the story. "That's the woman of my dreams. . . . She's all mine. Forever."

The plays themselves are Shepard's conversation with us. Beginning with *Curse*, the plays speak of the power of stories as well as their necessity and their limits. And we, the audience, speak in our minds back to Shepard, fitting his stories with our own as we learn to tell new ones, different ones.

Eddie told the truth, at least about writer and audience. "We'll always be connected."

Note

1.   Refers to the March 1983 *Harvard Advocate* interview concerning setting up established patterns then leaving such patterns. See Amy Lippman, in the Bibliography, p. 174, at the end of this collection.

NOTES ON *BURIED CHILD*

Jane Ann Crum

"... I feel like there are territories within us that are totally unknown. Huge, mysterious and dangerous territories."

—Sam Shepard
(Lippman 12)

ORIGINS: This essay grew out of my work as dramaturg on a production of *Buried Child* at Center Stage, Baltimore, Maryland, in April of 1986. In recognition of the collaborative nature of that production, I acknowledge the creative efforts of my colleagues, all of whom constitute the "we" in the article: Michael Engler, Director; Hugh Landwehr, Set Design; Catherine Zuber, Costume Design; James F. Ingalls, Lighting Design; and Stan Wojewodski, Jr., Artistic Director of Center Stage.

PLANNING: The known playwright and the unknown play

The mission was to bring the first production of a play by Sam Shepard to the Center Stage audience in Baltimore. Even though Shepard has been writing since 1964 and has been an "established" playwright since the late seventies, it isn't surprising that production of his works has lagged in the regional theater, where audiences are traditionally more conservative, and where season selections are heavily dependent on the classics. Because *Buried Child* had been awarded a Pulitzer Prize in 1979, it was sufficiently "respectable" to be accepted by Center Stage audiences, although critical minds appreciated the irony that only Shepard's movement toward a seemingly realistic framework enabled him to join the American playwrighting "establishment." Another mitigating factor leading to *Buried Child*'s acceptability is that, unlike its predecessor, *Curse of the Starving Class*, *Buried Child*'s sexuality and violence are disguised, hidden by broken beer bottles and a merely figurative act of rape. The fact remains that audiences are strangely more comfortable with broken incest taboos than with open acts of urination or male nudity. Finally, even though many in the audience might not have known Shepard's plays, they did have a familiarity with his film persona. Popular culture relentlessly appropriates the avant garde, and Shepard has moved from obscure dramatic innovator to recognizable film actor.

Since I begin my discussion with a pragmatic examination of audience expectations, let me suggest that one of the primary duties of the dramaturg is social accountability. Dramaturgs have been considered the conscience of the theater, and toward that end it is their duty to ask the "why" of the theatre—"why are we doing this play, here, and now?" The best definition of dramaturgy is to make drama work, a goal reached by seeing the theatrical process as a whole and asking fundamental questions about how that event can be made to resonate in contemporary society. Interpretation becomes an act of selection, but a selection that hinges on the mysterious communion between the text, the artist, and the audience. To be accountable, *Buried Child* must balance these factors. Toward that end, our first task was to find the essence of the Shepard landscape and then convey that essence to our audience. As we began work, the task became clearer: to make the strange familiar, and the familiar, strange.

ANALYSIS: Taking Measurements

The greatest resource for analyzing *Buried Child* is its obvious connections with dramatic realism as exemplified by Henrik Ibsen's *Ghosts* (Glore 63–65) and Eugene O'Neill's *Long Day's Journey into Night* (Cott 172). Like them, *Buried Child* concerns a son's homecoming and uses retrospective action to unravel a mystery in the past that controls the present. The structure is similar to Ibsen's reworking of the well-made play: namely, a three-act format with a climax in each act that occurs only minutes before each curtain, combined with continuous and mounting suspense. In visual terms, the

front room of an isolated Illinois farmhouse has its roots in Ibsen's
pallid parlors whose oppressive atmospheres exist in marked contrast to
the fjord vistas seen through its windows. Given these similarities, the
more interesting question for our production company was to
investigate *Buried Child*'s departure from its dramatic forebears.

One of the primary innovations of Shepard's dramaturgy is what
could be called tears in the fabric of reality. Such irregularities arise out
of seemingly inexplicable incongruities, e.g., Halie's change of clothes
between the first and third acts, the harvest of corn and carrots from an
unplanted field, and the questionable origins of the buried child. All
memories of the past become questionable as the difference between
offered information and buried information reveals itself. Terry
Eagleton, in his discussion of the relationship between subtext and text,
suggests that the subtext, which is "visible at certain 'symptomatic'
points of ambiguity, evasion or overemphasis" (Eagleton 178), is the
point where we, as readers (or, by extension, as audience) are able to
construct or "write" the text even if the novelist (or playwright) does
not. This point seems especially applicable to *Buried Child*'s portrayal
of four distinctly unconnected subjective realities (Halie's, Dodge's,
Tilden's and Bradley's). Two simultaneous principles are at work in
regard to the audience: (1) we gain pleasure from being able to construct
our own hypothesis as to the truth, but in doing so (2) we may miss
the point that what the text does not say and how it does not say it may
be the central clue to the playwright's "meaning."

As these ambiguities multiply, reality continually refuses to verify
itself and is revealed as malleable. Dodge seems closest to an awareness
that reality may be, in fact, unfixed. He rejects Shelly's idea that old
family photographs contain any semblance of truth:

Shelly: Your whole life's up there hanging on the wall. Somebody
          who looks just like you. Somebody who looks just like
          you used to look.
Dodge: That isn't me! That never was me! This is me. Right here.
          This is it. The whole shootin' match, sittin' right in front
          of you.

It would seem that the relationship between content and form
(Shepard's ability to balance on the edge of the irrational, while
remaining within the parameters of realism) suggests not only the
audience's difficulty in perceiving truth but also the playwright's refusal

to verify its existence. Returning to Eagleton's thesis, it becomes apparent that the pursuit of rational explanations for the gaps and contradictions of the text—in other words, to approach *Buried Child* as a mystery that must be unraveled—would only serve to reduce and domesticate the scope of Shepard's inquiry.

At this point, the rationale of the play's three-act structure becomes much more specifically related to Shepard's content. The problem has been to connect the seemingly disparate first act to the second and third acts, both of which concern the major issues of Vince's inheritance and the exhumation of the buried child. Seen in this light, beyond the obvious functions of establishing atmosphere and some minor exposition, the first act emerges as the means whereby the "strange" (the ambiguities, evasions, etc.) can become familiar. This Sunday is presented to us as any other Sunday following Tilden's return from New Mexico and is purposely ordinary so that the incongruities are established as standard procedure. It is only when Shelly enters in the second act that we experience a reversal of our previous expectations. Before Shelly's entrance, the audience must "write" the play in isolation. After her appearance, however, she serves as a mediator in the search for meaning and allows the audience an outlet for its frustrations as that meaning is continually denied.

Examine the corn sequence in Act I, when a completely mystifying occurrence, unplanted corn growing in a field left barren since 1935, is simultaneously questioned by Dodge, by Tilden, and by Halie. With scarcely a change in beat, Tilden brings a milking stool on stage and cleans the corn (which despite their denials, obviously exists) without further comment except for a later fight over the "mess" of the corn husks.) Strange, perhaps, but it is treated in such an understated manner that it elicits only a shrug, probably not a shock or a shudder. Yet when the question of Vince's identity is raised in the next act and both Dodge and Tilden treat the event of this prodigal son's return with even less consequence than the appearance of the corn, the strength of the parallel jars us back into a world that is not only strange, but dangerous. By the time Tilden puts on Shelly's fur coat (another proof of Tilden's connection with the world of nature or perhaps his sexual ambivalence) and begins to pace around her in ever-decreasing circles as he tells the story of the child's murder, Shepard has made the rational world recede, only to replace it with an irrational and terrifying landscape that takes us beyond sense and knowledge.

DESIGN: Arranging the terrain

In his study of Ibsen in *The Idea of a Theatre*, Francis Fergusson suggests that Ibsen's realistic scenography is balanced by the huge romantic landscapes of oceans, marshes, and snow-peaks that are glimpsed through the windows of "tasteless parlors" (157). This "exhilarating wilderness [that is felt] behind his cramped interiors," is indicative of the tension created between Ibsen's controlled human foreground and the wild freedom of the background. This same tension operates in *Buried Child*, but with the difference that the physical world undergoes the same process of excavation that accompanies the action within the room, and with the important distinction that in *Buried Child*, the background actually invades the foreground. Shepard's farm is not a passive constant, but functions actively as a harbinger of news, of messages from a primordial past when humanity was so attuned to the earth and its cycles that there was a psychological urgency for the shift of seasons. The progressions of the earth's produce that Tilden carries in his arms reflects the downward movement of the search for the child's identity: from the tall corn plant from which the ears are picked, to the carrot roots that are pulled out of the soil, to the corpse that Tilden must dig out of the ground.

> That corpse you planted last year in your garden
> Has it begun to sprout? Will it bloom this year?
> Or has the sudden frost disturbed its bed?
> Oh keep the dog far hence, that's friend to men,
> Or with his nails he'll dig it up again!

Functioning much as T. S. Eliot's "Dog" in *The Waste Land* childlike Tilden is the messenger who moves between foreground and background, bringing us tangible proof that the world outside the farm house is directly attuned to the events of the interior.

This gradual progression of ever-stronger visual imagery becomes a guidepost for design. The hardwood floor of set-designer Hugh Landwehr's room, warped by age and moisture and suggesting the shifting of the earth beneath it, is the color of bleached-bones, and contrasts starkly with Shelly's purple blouse, Bradley's yellow rain slicker, and the ears of pale green corn and orange carrots. Vegetables and actors alike drip with the water from the endless fall of real rain from the back of the porch roof. Halie's entrance in the third act with her arms full of two dozen long-stemmed roses adheres to Shepard's direction that "she is wearing a bright yellow dress, no hat, and white gloves," but the addition of a red wig, which is styled exactly as her white hair in the first act (and refers to Shelly's description of the "woman with the red hair" who holds the baby in the pictures upstairs), becomes an even stronger statement of the rejuvenating powers of the world outside. The huge staircase that Shepard so carefully describes as "with no landing" angled precariously into the catwalks above the audience, suggests not so much another part of the house, but an escape into another state of mind.

The visual world of the inside of the house is tersely described in stage directions as a couch, a television, a table with a lamp, and the staircase. Stripped of Victorian bric-a-brac, it could be an Ibsen parlor, with the exception of its walls. This is an easily missed detail, but Shepard's "walls" are a double wall of screens that run along the entire upstage wall and have the effect of bringing the out-of-doors into the interior of the house. Approaching the house for an entrance through the back-porch door, the characters appear as diffused shadows who gradually become clearly outlined on the porch, and don't attain sharp focus until they enter the room through the "solid interior door" specified by Shepard. This transition from shadow to light, from diffusion to focus, becomes especially ominous with Bradley's entrance in the first act. His limping, menacing bulk hovers over the figure of husk-covered Dodge, casting shadows that are pierced by a sudden gleam of light on his metal clippers as he bends to shave Dodge's head. By the time Vince makes his drunken entrance in the third act, the yellowish light of day transforms his body into an immense shadow puppet against the clear sky of morning.

Throughout the text, words such as "dissolve" and "disappear" are used to describe the processes of death and change. Vince's pseudo-military attack on the house takes place behind the screen and it is noteworthy that he cannot enter the room through the solidly realistic door, but must cut through the screen. He warns Shelley that the porch is "taboo territory," and that if she crosses onto the porch she will "disintegrate." "Dissolved" by the vision of himself in the window of his car (which echoes Halie's description of Ansel "disappearing" behind the glass of his car window), Vince reclaims his heritage with a Caesarean section of sliced metal. As he climbs onto the back of the couch, forcing Bradley off in the process, Halie and Father Dewis mount the stairs. Surveying the room while he stands on the back of the couch, Halie's words (which seem to have summoned his entrance with "Where are the men!"), bless his ascendancy as heir to the sofa/throne:

> **Halie:** I used to lie awake thinking it was all right if I died. Because Vincent was an angel. A guardian angel. He'd watch over us. He'd watch over all of us.

ENDINGS: Staging ambiguity

Shepard has been sharply criticized for his endings. The problems seem to stem from Shepard's professed dislike of traditional dramatic resolution:

> I think it's a cheap trick to resolve things. It's a complete lie to make resolutions. I've always felt that, particularly in theater, when everything's tied up at the end with a neat little ribbon and you're delivered this package. You walk out of the theater feeling that everything's resolved and you know what the play's about. So what? It's almost as though why go through all that if you're going to tie it all up at the end? It seems like a lie to me. (Lippman, 10)

The final consensus of those of us who worked with this particular product parallels a phrase that Shepard has used to describe *A Lie of the Mind,* but which seems especially applicable to the final tableaux of *Buried Child*—"a kind of awakening" (Cott 170). Regardless of the ambiguity of Vince's legacy (whether it be madness, drunkenness, violence, rebirth, ascension or fecundity) the term that best encompasses all possibilities is quite simply, change. What has existed in stasis has been re-energized. I believe that a perception that most changes are beneficial is a particularly American perspective, and Shepard claims this perspective when he asks his audience to enter into an unfixed reality, then frustrates their attempts to find meaning. What he offers instead, is the possibility of change.

Staging ambiguity necessitates the juxtaposition of all possibilities of meaning with an opposite, but equal, solution. To this end, the Center Stage production differed in one important aspect from Shepard's description of the final tableaux. Instead of placing the roses on Dodge's chest and then lying down on the sofa in an exact replication of Dodge's position at the end of Act One, our Vince wandered upstage to the screened wall, and with his back to the audience, looked upstage toward the fields envisioned by Halie in her disembodied monologue:

> **Halie:** . . . It's a miracle, Dodge. I've never seen a crop like this in my whole life. Maybe it's the sun. Maybe that's it. Maybe it's the sun.

As the soft homonym of sun/son lingered in the air, Tilden's ascent with the muddied bundle was complete, and in the silence that Shepard stipulates before the lights go to black, the final image was of complete neutrality—Vince, a faceless male silhouette, poised on the moment of awakening.

References

Cott, Jonathan. "The *Rolling Stone* Interviews Sam Shepard," *Rolling Stone* 490 (1987).

Eagleton, Terry. *Literary Theory: An Introduction*. University of Minnesota Press, 1983.

Fergusson, Francis. *The Idea of the Theatre*. Princeton University Press, 1949.

Glore, John. "The Canonization of Mojo Rootforce: Sam Shepard Live at the Pantheon," *Theater* 12.3 (1981).

Lippman, Amy. "Rhythm and Truths: An Interview with Sam Shepard," *American Theatre* 1.1 (1984).

Shepard, Sam. *Seven Plays*. New York: Bantam Books, 1984. All references to *Buried Child* will be from this edition.

CHARACTER BEHAVIOR AND THE FANTASTIC IN SAM SHEPARD'S *BURIED CHILD*

Bruce J. Mann

Perhaps the most striking feature of Sam Shepard's *Buried Child* (1978) is the behavior of its characters. Dodge, Halie, Tilden, Bradley, and Vince appear to be realistic enough as they play out this eery tale set in a Midwestern farmhouse. But time and again, they stop being even remotely predictable and either do something inexplicable or say something disturbing or irrelevant. What kind of dramatic characters are these? How can we explain a father who cannot recognize his own son, or a wife who speaks cheerfully to her husband moments after he confesses to having drowned and buried her baby? To understand the play, we need to determine the nature of Shepard's characters and the factors that animate their utterances and actions.

I will argue that these animating factors are not what we might expect, i.e., the characters' own psychological motivations. Instead, these factors are more exterior and issue from the rules of the literary mode Shepard employs in *Buried Child*—the fantastic mode. Dodge and Vince, therefore, are not Willy and Biff Loman of *Death of a Salesman*. In Arthur Miller's play, we probe the depths of the characters' psyches. In Shepard's play, however, the characters, although they are given memorable personalities, remain fairly shallow, and their behavior is

largely prompted by the exigencies of the mode. This does not mean
Shepard's accomplishment is any less impressive than Miller's. His
theatrical aim is just different. He does not want to explore a character's
psychological makeup; he wants to achieve an effect on his audience.
As I will discuss later, Shepard further enhances this effect of the
fantastic by building into his characters important elements of
American mythology, giving the play a special resonance.

Critics have not sufficiently addressed this question of the
characters' makeup and their quirky behavior. In a statement covering
several of Shepard's plays, including *Buried Child*, Ruby Cohn writes
that the play is "realistic in setting, straightforward in plot, and
coherent in character" (183). Gay Gibson Cima, in a provocative study,
emphasizes that Shepard composes his characters in a non-traditional
way, and insightful comparisons are drawn between the play's and
characters' structure and that of a modern art "combine" by Robert
Rauschenberg; nevertheless, Cima does not quite pinpoint the
characters' animating factors. The matter of characterization is not
directly addressed in Thomas Nash's fine study of the play's enactment
of the pattern of the Myth of the Corn King. And in their discussions,
Doris Auerbach and Milly Barrenger seem less concerned with the
characters' behavior *per se* than with what the play's action
communicates about American myths. All these commentaries
illuminate important aspects of the play, but none quite accounts for
the perception of one critic that "these characters . . . seem to be by
Hieronymus Bosch superimposed on Grant Wood" (qtd. in Auerbach
59).

Shepard's characters are indeed realistic American types (similar to
the figures in Grant Wood's painting, *American Gothic*). Yet their
actions carry them beyond the boundaries of normal behavior into the
realm of the irrational (hence, the allusion to Bosch). Stated another
way: These characters may not appear to differ markedly from, say, the
primitive, eccentric types Tennessee Williams created for *27 Wagons
Full of Cotton* or *The Unsatisfactory Supper*. But their behavior simply
does not resemble that of most realistic characters in modern American
drama. The following descriptions of Shepard's characters will attest to
this.

The family patriarch, Dodge, is a crusty, whisky-drinking, sickly
old farmer who does not recognize his grandson, Vince, when Vince
returns home after a six-year absence. Halie, Dodge's wife, is a

garrulous woman whose mind dwells on her family and religion; she concludes the play with enthusiastic remarks about the sun and opulent vegetation in the backyard, a peculiar thing to do because Dodge has just admitted to everyone that he killed the baby she conceived through an incestuous relationship years before with her son, Tilden. As for Tilden himself, he is a former All-American football player who acts like a gentle child, because "Something about him is profoundly burned out and displaced" (Shepard, *Buried Child* 69); at the end of the first act, he piles Dodge's sleeping body with corn husks. Tilden's brother, Bradley, is a mean-spirited amputee who cut off his leg in a chainsaw mishap; one of his first actions in the play is to shave Dodge's head while he sleeps, leaving bloody wounds on the scalp. Vince, Tilden's son, and Shelly, his girlfriend, are normal—if the word can be used—when we first meet them, and Shelly, who plays an important role in providing a sense of everyday reality, remains so. But Vince metamorphoses later and takes the house by storm to claim his inheritance.

These descriptions contain only a few of the behavioral eccentricities. Dodge and his family are constantly saying or doing something disturbing, unexpected, or inexplicable. An early example would be Halie's lengthy, nostalgic monologue about Ansel, another of her sons. In the initial portion of the speech, Halie praises Ansel as having been heroic and intelligent. Then suddenly the reminiscence takes on an unsettling tone as Halie recalls Ansel's wedding and mysterious death, apparently in a motel room during his honeymoon:

> The wedding was more like a funeral. You remember? All those Italians. All that horrible black, greasy hair. The smell of cheap cologne. I think even the priest was wearing a pistol. When he gave her the ring I knew he was a dead man. I knew it. As soon as he gave her the ring. But then it was the honeymoon that killed him. The honeymoon. I knew he'd never come back from the honeymoon. I kissed him and he felt like a corpse. All white. Cold. Icy blue lips. He never used to kiss like that. Never before. I knew then that she'd cursed him. Taken his soul. I saw it in her eyes. She smiled at me with that Catholic sneer of hers. She told me with her eyes that she'd murder him in his bed. Murder my son. (74)

Halie's bizarre outpouring comes across as ominous and even irrational. Whatever motivates her, in psychological terms, is not clear, nor is there an explanation for her attention turning, upon completion of the speech, to the corn Tilden has brought into the house. Her concern for Ansel's method of death evaporates, never to reappear, except vaguely in her statements about erecting an inane memorial statue for him. We in the audience are left scratching our heads and feeling uncomfortable, and not for the last time in the play. As a matter of fact, this feeling never disappears but is reinforced with every line, group of lines, or action.

What method is Shepard employing? Or is the behavior arbitrary? As I suggested above, what regulates the characters are the requirements of the play's literary mode—the fantastic. In a fantastic tale, according to Amaryll Beatrice Chanady (in her study of this mode in fiction), "two distinct levels of reality are represented," a world we accept as an everyday world, "ruled by laws of reason and convention," and a supernatural world, one that "is inexplicable according to our logic," and that appears to be "a breach of the normal order of things" (5). Throughout the tale, we must feel "the simultaneous presence of the real [everyday world] and the irrational [supernatural world]" (6), and this constant sense of "two conflicting codes in the text" is labelled "antinomy" by Chanady (12).[1] To maintain this ambiguous tension— and hence the effect of the fantastic—the realistic world must be maintained through such strategies as the introduction of realistic detail. Chanady points out that some authors include passages that serve little function other than to "provide an atmosphere of reality" (65). At the same time, the author cannot insert a supernatural event at the end of an otherwise realistic tale and thereby make it fantastic: "The structure and style of the narrative must develop the code of the uncanny, the inexplicable and disturbing, before the reader can be affected by the description of the supernatural event" (61). In addition, Chanady writes, a fantastic tale never resolves the antinomy between the levels of reality; the author provides no explanation, leaving the reader with a "reaction of uneasiness," or a sense of "uncertainty," because the "normal order" is never reestablished (123–124).

Buried Child conforms tightly to the mode's rules. The everyday world of the play is established, in part, by the farmhouse setting and the realistic-looking characters, and it is reinforced by the presence of realistic objects such as Dodge's liquor bottle, Tilden's chewing tobacco, Dodge's milking stool, the variety of rain protection (umbrella, slicker, newspaper, coat), Bradley's artificial leg, and the cup of beef bouillon, and also by real objects and places mentioned in the text (Dodge's farm implements listed in his last will and testament, and such places as New Mexico, Illinois, Iowa, and Los Angeles). Existing in antinomous tension with this world is a supernatural one, an aspect of the text some commentators omit from their discussions. (Nash's study, an exception, demonstrates the presence of this non-natural world.) This competing world is suggested by the play's title; as the tale develops, we may begin to wonder if the child Dodge murdered and buried years ago in the backyard is somehow exerting supernatural power. The strength of the everyday world's logic rules this out, but how else can the play's bizarre events be explained? Corn, potatoes, and carrots suddenly appear in the backyard after the field has lain fallow for decades. Vince, who spent younger days in the house, arrives, but neither Dodge nor Tilden recognize him. Even though it is incredible, the irrational possibility asserts itself that Vince is connected with the buried child and that he has been created (?) or drawn back (?) to the house to assume the patriarchal position Dodge will relinquish with his death. One cannot make sense out of it all, but this is precisely what Chanady describes as requisite for the effect of the fantastic.

The playwright's need to maintain antinomy between the two levels of reality motivates all of the characters' utterances and actions. If, at one moment, it is necessary to call attention to a real object, in order to reinforce the audience's belief in the reality and rules of this everyday world, then the character does so. Tilden, for example, interrupts his conversation with Dodge to ask if he can bring the milking stool into the living room; there is precious little motivation for the line other than the imperative of the mode. If, however, the realm of "the uncanny, the inexplicable and disturbing" needs reinforcement, then a character says something bizarre or acts in an irrational way. For instance, Halie's strange monologue on Ansel's wedding and subsequent death, quoted above, emerges not from any personal grief but instead from the need to maintain antinomy.[2] As the following survey of the plot illustrates, the entire script can be analyzed in terms of achieving this antinomous tension between two levels of reality.

The first image of *Buried Child* is antinomous. We see the "flickering blue light" of a television set with "no image, no sound," and Dodge sitting and staring at the screen (63); logic cannot entirely explain this. The pouring rain and Dodge and Halie's bickering, which initiates the play's action, seem realistic enough, but Shepard inserts material that is slightly out of kilter, such as Halie's consideration of whether taking pills is "Christian" (65). The rain, too, is antinomous, although we only realize this later; the rain could be interpreted as washing over the bones of the buried child, giving it second life. (The play's epigraph, from a Pablo Neruda poem, would support this interpretation: "While the rain of your fingertips falls, / while the rain of your bones falls, / and your laughter and marrow fall down, / you come flying.") Tilden then appears bearing armloads of corn from the backyard, to the disbelief of Dodge and Halie, and methodically shucks the corn, while sitting on a milking stool and chewing tobacco. To create more of a sense of the strange, the playwright includes many inconsistencies during the act: Tilden denies he was in "trouble" in New Mexico and forced to return home (70), a contradiction of his parents' accounts; Halie deplores the mess caused by the pile of corn husks even as she kicks them around the room (see Coe 153); and, after Halie leaves for a rendezvous with Father Dewis, Dodge, about to fall asleep, tells Tilden of the time Stan Musial hit a home run with the "Bases loaded. Runner on first and third," an impossibility (81).

The conclusion of the act intensifies the feeling of the supernatural in this realistic setting. Tilden completely covers Dodge's body, except for his face, with the corn husks, and then leaves, as if drawn by forces into the backyard. Bradley enters, cursing the rain, and after calling attention to the reality of his artificial leg, uses electric clippers to shave Dodge's head. Dodge thus becomes an emblem of the buried child which lies beneath the corn outside, although the audience only knows that something very odd is occurring.

The second act introduces Vince and Shelly, who seem to act normally and thereby sustain the code of the everyday world. Shelly, especially, performs a key role in the play's texture, because she serves as the audience's representative in this world, trying—just as the audience is—to figure out this family. Vince has returned to the house because he "has this thing about his family now," according to Shelly (86). But the code of the irrational soon asserts itself; Dodge does not recall ever having met Vince:

DODGE: . . . Who are you supposed to be?

VINCE: I'm Vince! Your Grandson!
DODGE: Vince. My Grandson.
VINCE: Tilden's son.
DODGE: Tilden's son, Vince.
VINCE: You haven't seen me for a long time.
DODGE: When was the last time?
VINCE: I don't remember.
DODGE: You don't remember?
VINCE: No.
DODGE: You don't remember. How am I supposed to remember if you don't remember? (89)

Tilden, who enters with an armful of carrots, does not recognize Vince either. Dodge matches this irrational event with an everyday concern, his need for a bottle of whisky to replace the one Tilden stole from him, and Vince finally agrees to go buy him one; he wants to use the trip to sort things out.

With Vince gone, Tilden confides to Shelly that Dodge once killed a baby and buried it somewhere. Dodge, whose strength is ebbing, overhears this and orders him to keep quiet, because the incident "happened before you were born! Long before!" (92). (Dodge makes this sound factual, but in the next act, he will imply that Tilden is the child's father!) The act concludes with Dodge incoherent, sitting on the floor and "moving his lips silently as though talking to someone invisible" (106). Bradley appears once again, and in a strange, cruel ritual, forces his fingers into Shelly's mouth. Afterwards, with the code of the irrational intensified again, Bradley drops Shelly's rabbit fur coat on top of Dodge, figuratively burying him a second time, presaging Dodge's upcoming death.

The final act opens in sunlight the next morning. The first image, of Shelly smiling as she brings Dodge a cup of beef bouillon, is unexpected, because Shelly should still be in shock after being terrorized by Bradley. She is, however, serene, and unaffected by Vince's continued absence. Shelly and Dodge converse, while Bradley sleeps on the couch, his artificial leg propped against it. Shelly tries to pursue the story of the buried child, but Halie returns, dressed now in yellow, not black, and she is escorted by Father Dewis, a Protestant minister with whom she has been drinking. Shepard introduces Dewis as a counterforce to the irrational events to come; through it all, Dewis acts as if this were only a family squabble. Halie keeps ignoring Shelly, who grows impatient and finally, to gain attention, smashes her cup and saucer against a wall and holds the leg of the now pathetic Bradley as hostage. "There isn't any reason here! I can't find a reason for anything," she exclaims (121). As audience members, we share her sentiments.

Shelly's pointed remarks about a family "secret" initiate Dodge's narration of the episode of the buried child, even though Shelly acts as if she would rather not hear it. Dodge's story of the incest and drowning ends at the precise moment that a drunken Vince vaults through the screen door of the porch. Then, while singing the Marines' Hymn, Vince smashes empty liquor bottles against the walls, an antinomous action because it uses a real object to create an uncanny effect. Vince responds irrationally to Shelly's greeting: "Who? What? Vince who? Who's that in there?" (125). He threatens everyone, calling himself "the Midnight Strangler! I devour whole families in a single gulp!" (126). Inexplicably, Halie recognizes Vince.

Vince cuts a hole in the porch's screen and dives through it into the living room, a stage emblem of birth, as if he were the buried child itself being reborn in order to take over control from Dodge. Immediately, Dodge announces that he will die momentarily and gives "his last will and testament" (128), a lengthy speech which serves the primary purpose of reestablishing "the atmosphere of reality," as Chanady dubs it. The speech, during which Vince is made Dodge's primary heir, is a catalogue of realistic items ("my spring tooth harrow, my deep plows, my disk plows, my automatic fertilizing equipment, my reaper, my swathe, my seeder, my John Deere Harvester . . .") (129). After this strangely moving episode, Shelly tells Vince she is leaving and acts surprised to hear that he will stay. "I've gotta carry on the line. I've gotta see to it that things keep rolling," he says, and he also tells her of his supernatural experience while driving the previous night (130). He says he watched his face while it was reflected in the windshield, and miraculously, that face transformed into the faces of his ancestors, back through time. Shelly leaves. Meanwhile, Halie has gone upstairs and Vince has thrown Bradley's leg offstage, forcing him to grovel after it. Then, Vince announces to Father Dewis that "There's nobody else in this house," a confusing statement (131). Finding that Dodge has died, Vince places Halie's roses, which he has been smelling, on Dodge's body and lies down on the couch, oblivious to the final, disquieting events.

From her upstairs room, Halie addresses Dodge, just as she did to open the play, and she acts as if absolutely nothing has happened since. She tells him that now she can see vegetables growing in the backyard, and as she speaks, the stage lights dim and Tilden comes into the living room, covered with mud from traipsing in the back yard. He carries the skeletal remains of the buried child and ascends the stairs to Halie's room as she finishes her monologue. True to the rules of the fantastic mode, the antinomy between the play's everyday and supernatural worlds is not resolved. We are left with an illogical situation. Are Vince and the buried child the same? If so, how can they both be seen onstage simultaneously? Has the child been supernaturally coordinating events, including Dodge's death and Vince's eery experience in the car? The logic of the play's everyday world (and ours) rules this out, but the play's supernatural world makes it impossible to explain away these events. We wonder what will happen when Tilden reaches Halie's room: Will she scream and ask Tilden to leave? Or will the child somehow assume control of things? The answer is not provided; only the unsettling effect of the fantastic remains.

This overview of *Buried Child* demonstrates the importance of the characters' behavior; this is Shepard's primary means of maintaining the tension between the two levels of reality and thereby achieving his desired effect. The characters reinforce one level of reality, only to switch suddenly to reinforce the other level. Consequently, performers of these roles must be sensitive to the words and actions called for at any one moment, and they must realize that the everyday world of the play deserves the same emphasis and embellishment that the irrational world does, even though the latter would *seem* to require more acting skills. What may appear to performers (and readers) to be meaningless realistic business—pulling on gloves, cutting carrots, manipulating an artificial leg, shaking off rainwater—requires masterful execution, because the audience must believe that this is a place where supernatural events cannot occur, although precisely those things do indeed *appear* to be happening here.

For actors and actresses, then, Shepard creates characters that present difficulties, but solvable ones; the characters' inconsistencies follow a pattern. But for American audiences, however, accustomed as they are to conventional realistic characters, Shepard's creations present more serious problems. These characters are not "complete," psychologically speaking, in the way that, say, Willy Loman is (and for Loman, we could substitute any number of more "complete" characters from the realistic plays of O'Neill, Odets, Williams, and Miller). To use terms Bert O. States has developed for discussions of the anatomy of dramatic character, Willy Loman has a Personality, a Character, and a clear Identity-project, whereas Shepard's characters have strong Personalities, fragments of Character, and simple Identity-projects. To clarify the terms: States describes Personality as that part of a dramatic character which distinguishes it from another—natural attributes which give the character its distinction (89). The element of Character consists of the dramatic figure's "value sphere as defined within or against that of society," its "system of internal self-government"; it "subsume[s] concepts like Freud's ego, id, and superego, the instincts, repressions, unconscious, and the like" (90–91). The third term, Identity, "is what attaches person, Character, and Personality to the world, like the foot of the mollusk" (96). Identity is the character's "project" in the play, his or her "thrust into the world of action" (96), and therefore, States speaks of characters having Identity-projects.

Before studying Shepard's characters, here is what the playwright himself has recorded about the creation of dramatic characters:

> In the writing of a particular character where does the character take shape? In my experience the character is visualized, he appears out of nowhere in three dimensions and speaks. He doesn't speak to me because I'm not in the play. I'm watching it. He speaks to something or someone else, or even to himself, or even to no one.
>
> I'm talking now about an open-ended structure where anything could happen as opposed to a carefully planned and regurgitated event which, for me, has always been as painful as pissing nickels. There are writers who work this way successfully, and I admire them and all that, but I don't see the point exactly. ("Visualization, Language . . ." 50)

In other words, the characters present themselves to Shepard's imagination as Personalities with Identity-projects. In what we might term a closed structure like *Death of a Salesman*, as opposed to Shepard's "open-ended structure," every move by Willy Loman is tied to his value scheme, his unnatural worship of his son, Biff, and his belief that such trivial things as being well-liked will deliver him the promises of the American Dream. The aim of the play is Character. Looking at Halie, on the other hand, we see flashes of Character behavior—in her feelings about Ansel's honeymoon, in her disdain for the way life is today, in her concern that Tilden stay inside—but these remain fragments which we cannot really assemble into a complete character like Willy Loman. Moreover, the Identity-projects are so limited—Dodge and his bottle, Tilden and the lure of the backyard, Bradley and his petty violence, and Halie and her rendezvous with Father Dewis—that these characters are almost comical in their structure, an element too few commentators mention; the play has a great deal of gallows humor.

Vince is not really an exception to the anatomy of Shepard's characters (although Shelly is, to some degree). Vince's abrupt and irrational transformation of Personality/Character at the end, which bothers Richard Gilman (xxvii), is similar, albeit on a larger scale, to the way the other characters behave (e.g., Halie's dropping of her concern for Ansel's wedding and death). To allow for his "open-ended structure," Shepard must have flexibility somewhere so that he can move characters from one type of behavior to another, as in Vince's case, to underscore the irrational code. The locus for this flexibility is the element of Character. In *Buried Child*, the demands of the fantastic mode create the conditions for behavior; the characters themselves lack the inner motors which reside in the Characters of realistic dramatic figures.

In addition to these observations, one final dimension of Shepard's characters deserves mention. Although the characters themselves are incomplete, each is imbued by the playwright with an important characteristic of American mythology. For example, Dodge makes several statements about drive and fortitude, and although he is the shadow of what he must once have been, we can still sense these attributes in him; drive is, of course, central to such conceptions as the American Dream. Halie's obsession with family, Tilden's affinity with the land, and Bradley's violence also mark out American mythological territory. More of it is covered in Vince's yearning for the values of small-town America, a yearning expressed by Shelly, too, when she compares the house, upon her arrival, to a "Norman Rockwell cover" (83). Shepard has Vince, in his transformed condition, synthesize the American mythological qualities of Dodge, Halie, Tilden, and Bradley, and he thus becomes an emblem of the American character and its concern with drive, violence, land, and family. Vince's rebirth/transformation suggests, at one level, the undying nature of the American character.

This subliminal strategy, of having characters reflect American myths, heightens our sense of the play's everyday world. We can identify it as an American world, as our world, which means the play is suggesting that the American experience itself is marked by the supernatural, the irrational, the disturbing, and the mysterious, a consequence of the national myths which shape us. With this strategy, Shepard is not endorsing the American character; he is simply calling attention to its disturbing implications. At the heart's core of America (the play is set in the middle of the country) are regenerative myths that defy everyday logic but that surface constantly to influence us.[3]

Shepard's vision leaves us thus unsettled in many ways, and the roots of this feeling can be traced to the unusual makeup and behavior of his characters. As we have seen, their unpredictable actions and incomplete structures make Dodge and his clan a strange group of figures who nevertheless rivet our attention. They do so because we are attracted by the aura of mystery which envelops them. We can account for the factors which animate their behavior, but as audience members, we cannot ultimately explain why these human figures onstage act the way they do. This is disturbing for us. Shepard has said that "A character for me is a composite of different mysteries. He's an unknown quantity. If he wasn't, it would be like coloring in the numbered spaces" ("Visualization, Language. . . ." 55). In *Buried Child*, the characters finally remain "unknown quantities"; we can never really come to know them as we do Willy Loman, and this contributes to our feelings of uncertainty. At the play's end, we cannot reduce these characters to a set of moral and ethical principles and thereby sum them up. What remains with us instead is the very experience of their behavior—the unsettling effect of the fantastic.

References

Auerbach, Doris. *Sam Shepard, Arthur Kopit, and the Off Broadway Theater*. Boston: Twayne, 1982.

Barrenger, Milly S. *Theatre Past and Present: An Introduction*. Belmont, California: Wadsworth, 1984, 471–74.

Chanady, Amaryll Beatrice. *Magical Realism and the Fantastic: Resolved Versus Unresolved Antinomy.* Garland Publications in Comparative Literature. New York: Garland, 1985.

Cima, Gay Gibson. "Shifting Perspectives: Combining Shepard and Rauschenberg," *Theatre Journal* 38.1 (1986): 67–81.

Coe, Robert. "Interview with Robert Woodruff," Marranca, 151–61.

Cohn, Ruby. *New American Dramatists: 1960–1980.* New York: Grove, 1982.

Gilman, Richard. Introduction, *Seven Plays.* By Sam Shepard. New York: Bantam, 1981.

Kleb, William. "Worse Than Being Homeless: *True West* and The Divided Self," in Marranca, 117–25.

Marranca, Bonnie, ed. *American Dreams: The Imagination of Sam Shepard.* New York: PAJ Publications, 1981.

Nash, Thomas. "Sam Shepard's *Buried Child*: The Ironic Use of Folklore," *Modern Drama* 26.4 (1983): 486–91.

Shepard, Sam. *Buried Child. Seven Plays.* New York: Bantam, 1981.

―――. "Visualization, Language and the Inner Library," *Drama Review* 21 (1977): 49–58. Rpt. as "Language, Visualization and the Inner Library" in Marranca, 214–19.

States, Bert O. "The Anatomy of Dramatic Character," *Theatre Journal* 37.1 (1985): 87–101.

Notes

1. The presence in *Buried Child* of realistic and non-realistic levels has been noted by several commentators, including Cima, Kleb, and Nash, although none argues as I do concerning the mode of the fantastic· and its dictation of characters' behavior patterns. Cima argues that the combination of the two levels causes the play to resemble Rauschenberg's "combines" (71). Kleb believes that Shepard's later play, *True West* (1980), successfully superimposes a subjective reality on an objective reality, whereas *Buried Child* does not (121). Nash claims that, as the play unfolds, it grows less realistic and more mythical.

2. Shepard has written that ". . . the power of words for me isn't so much in the delineation of a character's social circumstances as it is in the capacity to evoke visions in the eye of the audience. . . . Words as living incantations and not as symbols" ("Visualization, Language. . . ." 53). Thus, Shepard's dialogue aims at achieving an

effect on an audience instead of revealing a character's psychological depths.

3. Shepard writes that "the real quest of a writer is to penetrate into another world. A world behind the form" ("Visualization, Language. . . ." 55). In *Buried Child*, the playwright is penetrating into the "fantastic" world of myths and beliefs that underlie the American experience.

EXHAUSTION OF THE AMERICAN SOUL:
SAM SHEPARD'S *A LIE OF THE MIND*

Ron Mottram

A Lie of the Mind is a play of disturbing contradictions. Its characters leave home despite their desperate need for home; they forget the past even though the present is controlled by it; they are most alone when in the company of those they love; they look for truth in self-constructed lies. They are as much prisoners of an unjust fate as was Oedipus, but since they live in a world shorn of the gods, their tragedy may be little more than absurdity. In their actions they echo St. Paul's lament, "The good that I would, I do not: but the evil which I would not, that I do." The stunning paradox of their lives is that they are inextricably bound together but seem inevitably destined for separation. Ironically, the common denominator between Shepard's characters is their essential estrangement from each other.

These are familiar ideas in Shepard's work, especially in the "family trilogy," *Curse of the Starving Class, Buried Child*, and *True West*, and in *Fool for Love*. Nowhere, however, are Shepard's obsessions more forcefully exhibited than in *A Lie of the Mind*. Here is a writer at his full powers, probing the wounds that people inflict on each other, especially those inflicted by men on women. In their inability to fashion lasting commitments and to escape an inborn

wildness and violence, the male characters cause pain and rend the fabric
of family life. They generate lasting antagonisms in their wives and
stunt the development of their children. Finally, they leave home, as
Lorraine, one of the two wife-mothers in the play, puts it in relation to
her own husband, chasing "some mystery he doesn't even have a clue
to."

Shepard introduces the published version of the play with a
quotation from Peruvian writer Cesar Vallejo which proposes a
fundamental contradiction and sets the stage for the situation that opens
the play: "Something identifies you with the one who leaves you, and
it is your common power to return: thus your greatest sorrow.
Something separates you from the one who remains with you, and it is
your common slavery to depart: thus your meagerest rejoicing." This
dialectic of identification and separation is found at the outset in the
first stage direction which calls for the "impression of huge dark space
and distance between the two characters" and in a set design that allows
the simultaneous existence of two locations, and thus a comparison of
the actions that occur in them, while it suggests that the space between
them is purely mental and largely unbridgeable.

At the heart of the contradiction in the relations between men and
women is a basic difference in their natures. Meg, the other wife-mother
in the play, states it clearly, if too simply, when she says to her
husband, Baylor: "The female—the female one needs—the other. . . .
But the male one—doesn't really need the other. . . . He needs
something else. But he doesn't know what it is." Although Baylor at
first reacts as if he doesn't understand what Meg is talking about, he is
finally prodded into revealing a basic feeling of entrapment and a desire
for a life in some mythical Eden in the wilderness: "I could be up in the
wild country huntin' Antelope. I could be raising a string a' pack mules
back up in there. Doin' somethin' useful. But no, I gotta' play a
nursemaid to a bunch a' feeble-minded women down here in
civilization." Baylor does not leave, but in the case of the men who do,
flight usually leads to an alienation no less engulfing than the one
experienced at home.

As the play begins, the principal motivating event of the narrative
has already occurred: Jake has beaten his wife, Beth, so badly that he
thinks she is dead. It was an act over which he seems to have had no
control; he is surprised he did not see it coming. All other actions are
focused by this seminal event, even those that do not directly stem from

it. Discussions of the past, for example, dredge up information that sheds light on Jake's mental condition and physical behavior and link his actions to the violence and instability of his father, typical of a Shepard character. The nature of both families is explored as the various family members react to the beating and position themselves in relation to Beth and Jake. Like the buried child of Shepard's earlier family study, the beating serves to clarify long hidden and suppressed thoughts and feelings.

That which is hidden and needs to be discovered is always at the mercy of memory, a faculty that for Shepard's characters is selective at best. Repeatedly, they claim not to remember people and events. Typical is a scene between Lorraine and Jake in which he cannot remember his childhood room, even when he is in it, but does remember that his father's ashes were put in a box and kept by the family. Lorraine responds with the question, "Now, how can you remember somethin' like that and not remember this room?" Jake's answer is an unreflective evasion: "Some things stick in your mind." Later, Jake comments to his sister, Sally: ". . . There's a possibility that you could do something that you didn't even know about. You could be somewhere that you couldn't even remember being." Perhaps. But the title of the play implies that this apparent trick of the mind is really a lie of the mind and that lying to oneself and others is unavoidable. When Frankie, Jake's brother, tries to see Beth, he is driven off by her brother, Mike. Beth does not believe Mike, however, when he says that it was not Jake who was trying to see her. Mike responds in anger: "Well, goddamnit! She wants to know the truth. She says—'tell me the truth, you're lying to me.' I tell her the truth and she turns it into a lie." A short time later Baylor, Beth's father, demands that she be told the truth about her injuries. "Everyone's been tiptoeing around here like she can't handle the plain truth," he complains. But Baylor also has a hard time handling the truth and is subject to his own lies of the mind.

Closely linked to the lies that the characters tell each other and themselves are the secrets, real and imaginary, that help govern their lives. Most potent are the secrets of the past, especially the darkest of them all, the role that Jake played in the death of his own father. Although she had sworn to Jake never to reveal what had happened, Sally finally tells Lorraine the whole story. In clearly Oedipal terms she insists that Jake set up the condition that led to his father's death on the road. Although Lorraine tries to dismiss the death as an accident, Shepard has already established in the text that it was as much "fated" to happen as was Oedipus' killing of his father. Sally had seen in both father and son what she describes as "a terrible meanness that was like—murder almost." When Sally tried once to help her father who had fallen on the road, he turned this murderous quality on her: "I saw it in his eyes. This deep, deep hate that came from somewhere far away. It was pure, black hate with no purpose." Sally's further insistence that Jake had known what he was doing because he made her promise never to tell Lorraine elicits a response that completes the Oedipal allusion. Lorraine's denial that Jake is a murderer gives way to a counter accusation that it was Sally who really killed the father because she did nothing to help him. As the scene ends, the mother-daughter conflict subsides, however, and Lorraine wishes for an Artaud-like purification: "You know what I miss more than anything now? . . . The wind. One a' them fierce, hot, dry winds that come from deep out in the desert and rip trees apart. You know, those winds that wipe everything clean and leave the sky without a cloud."

For Shepard the past cannot be simply swept clean. *A Lie of the Mind*, however, provides, for the first time in Shepard's work, a suggestion that apparently ingrained male hate and violence might be healed. In the most extraordinary scene in the play, Beth, who has herself been almost destroyed by this hate and violence, confronts Jake's brother Frankie with two possibilities: castration (metaphorically presented as the amputation of his leg which has been injured by another act of male violence) or the feminizing of his consciousness. Using a theatrical metaphor (Shepard suggests that the theater is a possible route to understanding and change) Beth identifies Baylor's shirt as a costume and presents herself as a man by putting on the shirt. She then suggests that Frankie be a woman and together they can make a life. This playacting first reveals the male attitude which sees woman as not being complete without man (part of the Eve myth). As Frankie resists Beth's "male" advances, she interprets his actions and makes clear the nature of the distorted male perspective: "You fight but all the time you want my smell. You want my shirt in your mouth. You dream of it. Always. You want me on your face." Beth then asks Frankie to pretend to be Jake, but with a difference: "But soft. With me. Gentle. Like a woman-man." By imaginatively assuming the characteristics and place of a woman, Frankie-Jake can transform himself: "You could be better. Better man. Maybe. Without hate. . . . You could pretend so much that you start thinking this is me. You could really fall in love with me. . . . Us. In a love we never knew." Frankie's imagination fails, however. Unable to make the leap, he wants to leave; Beth returns to the castration image and questions the ultimate act for the Shepard male who fails. "You can only think of far away?" she asks. "Nothing here? Nothing right here? Now."

Beth is the central character of the play. She is not only the victim of Jake's aggression, and so is at the heart of the play's principal event, but, like Cassandra, the one with the clearest vision and the one with the most to lose. If the characters can be seen as tragic, hers is the greatest tragedy. As the play draws to a close, she slips farther into isolation until finally Meg and Baylor are no longer even aware of her presence. At first Meg laments the change for the worst, complaining that Beth is so young. To this Baylor responds with a fatalistic view that places not only Beth but all humans in a position that is more absurd than tragic: "I know she's young. What's that got to do with it? You think the powers that be hang around waiting for the right time, the right moment to bear down on us? . . . They could give a shit about her predicament or any of us. We're all gonna' get clobbered when we least expect it."

Although this may be the general human condition, the powers that be are often concrete, especially for the women in the play. In one of her conversations with Frankie, Beth insists that her brain has been cut out: "No brain. Cut me out. Cut. Brain. Cut." On the most immediate level, of course, this refers to Beth's confusion as to what happened to her and obviously cannot be taken literally. Frankie's response, however, is naively literal: "They wouldn't just go in there and operate without your consent. They can't do that. It's a law. They need written consent or something. Somebody has to sign something." Beth's answer to this remark, that Mike did the signing, surely shifts the image to the level of metaphor and refers not to the physical damage caused by Jake's beating but to the psychic damage inflicted on her by her brother and father in her growing up.

Typical of Shepard's fathers, Baylor dominates Meg and Beth, treating them with a contempt based on his desire to be free of obligations. Meg confronts him over this issue: "You think it's me, don't you? . . . You think your whole life went sour because of me. Because of mother. Because of Beth. If only your life was free of

females, then you'd be free yourself." In a rage that Meg has spoken up,
Baylor admits to these feelings, only to be contradicted by Meg's
suggestion that he go off on his own and leave the women to take care
of themselves, something they have been doing all along anyway.

Baylor stays, but Lorraine's husband has long since left his family.
"Is there any good reason in this Christless world why men leave
women?" asks Lorraine. "Isn't there enough to suffer already? We got
all kinda' good reasons to suffer without men cookin' up more." When
Sally suggests that he cannot be condemned anymore since he is dead,
Lorraine explodes in a vehement retort: "I'll condemn him right up to
my last breath! He shaped my whole life. Vengeance is the only thing
that keeps me goin'. . . . He's still alive in me. You understand that?
He's still walkin' around inside me. He put stuff into me that'll never
go away. Ever. He made sure a' that."

These errant husbands' poisoning of their wives through resentful
domination and abandonment is finally less destructive than Mike's
more subtle attack on Beth's identity. By assuming that he knows what
is best for her, he goes beyond the bounds of protector and even of
brother and seeks to absorb her into himself. His apparent concern for
her and desire to save her further pain is progressively revealed to be a
dismissal of her own judgement and a disregard for her individual worth.
As Beth resists this manipulation, Mike's initial tenderness turns to
violent force and finally to his own abandonment of the family. Mike's
actions and feelings are presented as a travesty of Beth's call for a man
whose sympathies and imagination are broad enough to find the woman
in himself. Appropriately, Beth states the problem when she first
returns to the family home: "You make an enemy. In me. In me! An
enemy. You. You. You think me. You think you know. You think.
You have a big idea. You—You have a feeling. You have a feeling I'm
you. I'm not you! This! (Points to her head.) This didn't happen to
you. This! This. This thought. You don't know this thought. How?
How can you know this thought? In me." Like Lorraine, Meg moves to
the defense of her son and tells Beth that Mike is only trying to help.
Beth sees clearly, however, and goes to the heart of the issue: "But he
lies to me. Like I'm gone. Not here. Lies and tells me iz for love. Iz
not for love! Iz pride!" Ultimately, Beth loses the battle for recognition
as Mike leaves without ever acknowledging her wishes or point-of-
view, and Meg and Baylor become insanely absorbed in folding an
American flag, oblivious to Beth's needs and Jake's arrival. Here, in

Beth's predicament, we see what may be the most destructive of the lies of the mind in Sam Shepard's play, that one which enables men to render women invisible, a violence far worse than Jake's.

One of the great strengths of *A Lie of the Mind* is its structural integrity. As the action switches back and forth between the two distinct sections of the set, characters, dialogue, elements of the mise en scène, and even whole scenes are paralleled and contrasted. In Act I, for example, Scene 2 between Mike and Beth in the hospital room is mirrored by Scene 3 between Frankie and Jake in the motel room. Scene 4 completes the set by returning to Mike and Beth. Scene 5 adds Lorraine and Sally to the motel room and presents their first contact with Jake, while Scene 6 brings Baylor and Meg to the hospital to see Beth. Similar relationships exist between scenes throughout the play.

On a more detailed level, an intricate web of interlocking actions, stage directions, and language identifies the characters with each other even while they remain separated in their own spaces. The following inventory, in the form of a chart, specifies some of these interconnections and is meant to be suggestive of the play's overall richness.

CHARACTERS ACT/SCENE   DIALOGUE/ACTION

Mike/Beth   Act I, Scene 2   Beth's talking to Mike in hospital room soon after she has been beaten by Jake.

Beth: ' "Don' leave me."
Mike: "I won't honey. I promise."

Frankie/Jake   Act I, Scene 3   Frankie and Jake in motel room soon after the beating incident.

Jake: "Just sit with me for a while. Stay here."
Frankie: "Okay."

Mike/Beth   Act I, Scene 2   Stage direction: Mike stands... stroking her back.

Frankie/Jake   Act I, Scene 3   Stage direction: Frankie stands behind couch with a plastic bag full

of ice, trying to apply it to the back
of Jake's neck.

Jake/Frankie   Act I, Scene 3   Jake talking to Frankie about Beth.
Jake: "Like my whole life is lost from losing her."

Beth/Mike   Act I, Scene 4   Beth explaining her relationship to
                                    Jake.
Beth: "Heez in me... HEEZ MY HAAAAAAAAAAAAAAAART!!"

Lorraine/Sally   Act III, Scene 1   Lorraine talks about her dead
                                    husband.
Lorraine:". . . he's still alive in me . . . He's still walking around
inside me."

Jake/Frankie   Act I, Scene 3   Jake walks around motel room
                                    delivering monologue at rapid
                                    speed.

Beth/Mike   Act I, Scene 4   Beth slowly walks in circles around
                                    hospital room.

Beth/Mike   Act I, Scene 4   Beth trying to walk, "breathing hard
                                    from the effort."
Jake/Lorraine   Act I, Scene 7   Jake at home with Lorraine,
                                    "gasping for breath."

Jake   Act I, Scene 3   Stage direction: Jake suddenly falls
                                    to the floor, collapses.
Beth   Act I, Scene 4   Stage direction: Suddenly she pulls
                                    away from Mike, takes a few steps
                                    on her own and falls.

Jake/Frankie   Act I, Scene 3   Jake's response when Frankie tries to help him get up.

Jake: "Just get away!"

Beth/Mike   Act I, Scene 4   Beth's response to Mike as he tries to hold her up.

Beth: "DON' TUSH ME!"

Beth   Act I, Scene 4   Stage direction: Beth just stands there for a while staring at her feet.

Jake   Act I, Scene 7   Stage direction: He just stares at his feet.

Lorraine/Sally   Act I, Scene 5   Lorraine's response when Sally tells her about Jake's possibly killing Beth.

Lorraine: "Who's Beth?"

Meg/Mike   Act I, Scene 6   Meg's response when Mike tells her that Jake has beaten up Beth.

Meg: "Who's Jake?"

Jake   Act I, Scene 5   Stage direction: Jake rolls over slowly, facing out toward audience now.

Beth   Act I, Scene 6   Stage direction: Beth suddenly rolls over facing audience.

Jake/Frankie   Act I, Scene 3   Jake describes Beth's acting and questions whether it was "just pretend."

Lorraine/Frankie   Act I, Scene 5   Lorraine's comment on Jake's behavior.

Lorraine: "He's just play-acting. . . . It's all pretend."

Lorraine/Frankie Act I, Scene 5   Lorraine's description of Jake.
Lorraine: "Every time he gets near liquor he thinks it's his God
              given duty to keep pace with his old man."

Meg/Beth   Act II, Scene I   Meg's description of Mike.
Meg: "Honey, I can't ask Mike. You know how he gets. He gets
        just like your father."

Lorraine/Jake   Act I, Scene 7   Lorraine's   description   of   her
                                   husband's actions.
Lorraine:"Those were the days we chased your Daddy from one air base
          to the next."

Meg/Mike   Act II, Scene 1   Meg talks about Baylor.
Meg: "Sometimes I think he's hiding from us."

Jake/Lorraine   Act I, Scene 7   Jake cannot remember his room.

Beth/Meg   Act II, Scene 1   Beth cannot remember her room.
Beth: "This—This—This is where I used to be?"

Beth   Act II, Scene 1   In   response   to   Meg   offering
                                     slippers.
Beth: "My feet are fine."

Jake   Act II, Scene 2   Trying to keep his mind off Beth.
Jake: "Don't think about her feet."

Beth/Mike   Act II, Scene 1   Beth: "You think me. You think
                                     you know. . . . You have a feeling
                                     I'm you."

Mike/Frankie	Act II, Scene 1	Mike: "Far as I'm concerned you and your brother are the same person."

Baylor/Meg	Act II, Scene 1	Baylor stops Meg from helping Beth.

Baylor: "Let her do it. She can do it. 'Bout time she starts doin' things by herself."

Jake/Sally	Act II, Scene 2	Jake describes incident from the past when his father stopped Lorraine from helping Sally.

Jake: ". . . listening to him bellowing down the hallway at Mom. Warning her not to go in and help you out."

	Act II, Scene I	Sound cue: the sound of a dog defending his territory is heard in the distance.
	Act II, Scene 2	Stage direction: Jake and Sally look up and stare at each other like two dogs with their hackles up.
Beth/Mike	Act I, Scene 2	Beth: "Yore the dog. Yore the dog they send."

Jake/Frankie	Act I, Scene 1	Referring to Beth.

Jake: "She's dead!"

Beth/Mike	Act III, Scene 3	Referring to Jake.

Beth: "He's dead."

Although *A Lie of the Mind* focuses on two families and only eight characters, it paints a broad canvas. In it we see an exhaustion of the American soul produced by an internecine battle among those who should most love each other and yet, for almost inexplicable reasons, seem least capable of doing so. Shepard has revealed a culture that has run out of places to go and must now look deep into itself to find a cure for its discontents. The frontier of irresponsibility is no longer available as an escape. Running off to the wilderness leads only to death, as does a blind lashing out at the constraints imposed by close interactions with other people. Everything that Shepard has been doing in his writing for the past decade has led up to this profoundly unsettling description of the American condition. Whether there is place in Shepard's work for a healing of this exhaustion remains to be seen.

Reference

Sam Shepard. *A Lie of the Mind*. New York and Scarborough, Ontario: New American Library, 1986. (All quotations are from this text.)

LANGUAGE AND DESIRE: THE ABJECT IN SHEPARD'S *RED CROSS*

Leonard Wilcox

Red Cross (1968) remains one of the most enigmatic of Sam Shepard's early plays. The lights suddenly snap on and the unsuspecting audience is momentarily snow-blinded by the antiseptic whiteness of the stage set. The setting is putatively a vacation retreat, a mountain cabin set in a complex of rustic chalets (complete with tennis courts) in a mountain wilderness; yet with its spartan twin beds it could be a hospital, a private sanatorium for the diseased, an asylum for those with more than physical illness. The ambiguity of the setting, the dream-like fantasies of the three characters, are not all that make the play bizarre and uncanny: one of the characters skis on a bed; another blithely announces he has been infected with genital crabs for some ten years, and there is an extended swimming lesson conducted on adjacent beds. And the conclusion, a stream of blood running down the male character's forehead—and then the sudden blackout—is so powerful as to make audiences gasp (Levy 96).

Yet little work has been done on *Red Cross* to explore its provocative ambiguity. Nor in spite of its obvious dream-like qualities and its profoundly unsettling effects, has the play been explored on a psychological level. Michael Bloom, in discussing Shepard's early plays, has characterized them as "a gestalt theater which evokes the existence behind behavior," and connects Shepard's early plays with the late sixties spirit, particularly Norman O. Brown's call for embracing the madness of the Dionysian spirit and the apocalyptic which proceeds by dreams, visions, and hallucinations (Bloom 72). But in spite of this acknowledged link between these plays and the world of dream, hallucination, and madness little has been done to connect them, for example, with Freud or the post-Freudians.

Shepard's *Red Cross* in fact seems to invite comparison with Freud's *Interpretation of Dreams*. Like the Freudian dream the play might be seen as having a manifest and latent content; like the Freudian dream, the "dream content" is not to be found in the dream thoughts, but rather as Freud described it, "centered elsewhere" (Freud 336). It is a play that superbly illustrates the principles of condensation and displacement. Jim's crabs, for example, are condensed and overdetermined symbols of sexual desire, sexual torment, and existential travail. Sexual desire and sexual intercourse are comically displaced as Jim and the maid swim on adjacent beds, while Jim urges her on: "That's good. It's good when it hurts. It's working then. Keep it up. We've almost got it" (Shepard 117). Moreover, like the Freudian dream the play is replete with verbal and visual puns: bed changing becomes a physical ordeal in which the positions of the beds are changed on the stage.

Yet the model of the Freudian dream, with its hermeneutical core, organized around the phenomenon of wish fulfillment, does not illuminate the extent to which the play is concerned with the instability of the symbolic order, the slippage between the signifier and the signified, the mismatch between language and desire. It is not only that the setting of the play is profoundly ambiguous. It is not simply that Jim and Carol, the "vacationing" couple, have a strangely impersonal relationship and that they drift off into their fantasies at various points, or that Carol, at the outset of the play, exhibits neurotic and hysterical symptoms which "float" from her wrists to her nose and back to her feet, which she speculates could be caused by "anything," such as "beer, or water or too many cigarettes." More than these factors there is a radical disjunction between context and monologue, between words and actions. It is as if words themselves have become detached from things, that the signifiers in the play float unattached from anything real, or that they form a chain of contiguous elements that are related metonymically, propelled by desire from object to object, never finding full and present satisfaction. In this sense the signifiers of the play function not simply in the way they might in a Freudian dream, censoring, condensing and displacing a "latent" content but, more in terms of a Lacanian model of desire, in which desire (and the language which constitutes it) can find no final signifier or object because that final object of desire—the imaginary harmony between the mother and the world—has been lost forever.

Part of this sense of desire in language as a continual deferral, as an impossibility of satisfaction, is evoked by metamorphosis and mutations of the central images, and in the utterances of the characters which form a network of displacement. The "little red splotch of blood and a whole blanket of white snow" in Carol's initial skiing fantasy is transformed into the enigmatic image of blood on Jim's forehead at the end of the play; her fantasy that her "head will blow up" is realized (but not given definitive meaning) in the horrifying image of blood running down Jim's forehead just before the lights black out. Jim's remark in his swimming fantasy that "your body stays warm inside. Its just the outside that gets wet" becomes the maid's statement that "once you get used to your flippers and fins and your new skin, then it comes very easy." Carol's vision of mastery in her skiing fantasy, "Everything will be working at once," is transformed in the context of Jim's swimming instructions, "you're becoming more concerned with one end or the other rather than the collaboration of the two as a total unit." And Carol's rampaging and disastrous descent down the snowy hill becomes the maid's descent into the quiet oceanic depths where "rolling and yelling" is replaced by "diving and floating." Desire becomes in some sense analogous to Carol's floating hysterical symptoms which range across her body: it moves restlessly, from signifier to signifier, across the textual body of *Red Cross*, never finding full and present satisfaction, just as language itself can never be seized as full presence or definitive meaning.

Red Cross is thus concerned with the unsettled movement of desire and the way in which unconscious drives impinge on the symbolic order. The restless and unsettled movement of desire is manifest in *Red Cross*, as it is in other Shepard plays, in a world where characters spin out fantasies, attempting to displace or subsume the fantasies of other characters. In these verbal contests, language is stripped of its referentiality, and reduced to exchange value in a struggle of desire and power. But this play of desire, ultimately related to the instability of language, is evident on another level in the play: in its theme of abjection. For abjection is at the heart of the play, in Jim's loathsome and disgusting infection of crab lice which threaten to take over the body, moving up from the genital region to the navel, to the armpits and hair. Here Julia Kristeva's notion of the abject might be useful. Kristeva theorizes that the abject threatens the stability of the subject and the symbolic order itself by radically problematizing inner and outer, self and not self, and by holding out the possibility of regressing to the entropic and undifferentiated. Moreover for Kristeva the abject prefigures the Oedipus complex and the castration anxiety which accompanies entry into the symbolic order and thus plays a role in delineating two competing realms we see operating in Shepard's play— the maternal, preverbal and "semiotic," and the paternal, phallic functions of language.

In her *Powers of Horror*, Kristeva examines the phenomenon of abjection in patriarchal society and analyses the ways in which it functions to separate the human from the non-human, and the fully constructed subject who has entered the symbolic order from the partially formed subject who has yet to do so. The abject is most often culturally defined in terms of religious abominations—sexual perversity, incest, corporal alteration, decay and death; often it has to do with corpses, bodily waste (blood, shit, urine, pus), the female body, and menstrual blood. For Kristeva the place of the abject is the place where meaning collapses, the place where "I" is not. But the exclusion of the abject substance (whether expelled from the body and deposited safely on the other side of an imaginary border where "I" is not, or culturally defined in religious ritual as "taboo") is necessary to guarantee that the subject take up his/her place in relation to the symbolic. For individuals and social groups constitute themselves in the symbolic order through difference—what they are not (Kristeva, *Powers* 2).

Moreover, part of the construction of the subject in the symbolic order has to do with the Oedipus complex, for the abject is often associated with the figure of the mother. Kristeva notes that in religious ritual the figure of the mother becomes an abject the moment the child rejects her in favor of the father who represents the symbolic order. Thus the cultural construction of abjection serves to prepare the subject for entry into the symbolic order by breaking ties with the mother.

Besides placing prohibitions on the maternal body, rituals of defilement also serve to ward off fears of sinking irretrievably into the maternal body. Polluting objects in these rituals—which are prohibitions against contact with the mother—fall into two categories: external (decay, infection, disease, corpse) and internal (menstrual blood). Menstrual blood relates to the mother in an obvious way, but the former are linked to the mother because of her role in sphincteral training. This is the child's first contact with authority, and the context in which the child learns about its body: that which is clean and unclean. This process of the "primal mapping of the body" Kristeva calls the "semiotic," which is associated with the maternal function as opposed to the paternal:

> Maternal Authority is the trustee of that mapping of the self's clean and proper body; it is distinguished from paternal laws within which, with the phallic phase and the acquisition of language, the destiny of man will take place. (*Powers* 72)

The distinction between maternal authority and paternal law is crucial: Kristeva argues that maternal authority is characterized by the exercise of authority without guilt, and associated with a time of fusion with mother and nature. But the paternal order, or the symbolic, inaugurates "a totally different universe of socially signifying performances"(Kristeva, *Powers* 74) where embarrassment, shame, guilt, and desire come into play—-the order of the phallus. Thus images of abjection which are central to our culturally constructed notions of the horrific signify a split between two orders: the maternal authority and the law of the father.

Yet the realm of abjection is profoundly ambiguous on several levels. Although the abject, which threatens life, must be excluded, it must also be tolerated, for as the "other" it also defines life. Moreover, (like the Freudian death instinct) it provokes the horror as well as the attraction of the undifferentiated. The abject in the form of body wastes, for example, is experienced as horrific and threatening to the integrity of the subject who has gained access to the (paternal) symbolic order and therefore construes (or rather misconstrues) his identity as whole, complete, and constituted in opposition to the other, the abject (not I); on the other hand it fascinates and attracts precisely because it points back to a time of primal unity between subject, mother, and nature, and a time when body wastes produced no shame. Ultimately the abject is radically ambiguous because it threatens to cross the border between the human and nonhuman, or throw the border into question. Thus as Kristeva points out, the abject is that which does not "respect borders, positions, rules" . . . that which "disturbs identity, system, order" (Kristeva, *Powers* 4). This notion illuminates a variety of texts including the horror film, a genre from which Shepard drew inspiration. As Barbara Creed points out; in the horror film "the function of the monstrous remains the same—to bring about an encounter between the symbolic order and that which threatens its stability" (Creed 49).

These central ideas, that abjection throws into question the stability of the symbolic order, that it "disturbs identity, system, and order," and that it is related to the prohibition of incest all seem particularly relevant for a play like *Red Cross*. Images of abjection are introduced at the outset in Carol's speech: blood, a broken, mutilated, and decapitated body (the neck reduced to a "bloody stump"), and the corpse itself being fed upon by "some blue jay." But the central image of the loathsome and abject is to be found in Jim's crab-lice infested body. The lengthy scene without dialogue in which Jim meticulously picks his crabs, squashing them on the floor, often evokes laughter from an audience, but it also evokes sensations of itching and often provokes scratching, suggesting the degree to which body lice threaten the "clean and proper" subject and are, like all things abject, to be relegated to the "not I" and expelled. Jim, who has "had crabs for about ten years now," displays something of the abjection of self found in mystical Christendom: he is a self-styled ascetic submitting his body to scourging by a living and motile hair shirt. Yet if the mystical Christian turned his abjection of self into proof of humility before God, Jim is neither humble nor godly, but rather narcissistically caught up in fantasy and physical exercise. Moreover, Jim's genital crabs suggest the abhorrent blurring of distinctions between host and parasite, animal and human. For him crabs do not constitute an other to be ejected or repelled; rather they collapse the boundaries between the human and animal body: for Jim having crabs is merely like "having two bodies to feed." Kristeva quotes George Bataille who links abjection "with the inability to assume with sufficient strength the imperative act of excluding" (Kristeva, *Powers*), and such seems to be the case with Jim who merely finds the pestilence visited upon him "kind of fun."

If Kristeva is right, abjection not only at once delineates and problematizes the border between self and not-self, but it is related to prohibition placed on the maternal body as a defense against incest. Abjection, especially that in which parts of the mother or maternal body is constituted as abject, helps the subject break away from the maternal and enter the paternal symbolic order; yet insofar as the maternal as abject is fascinating and ambivalent, it is deeply bound up with Oedipal yearnings. *Red Cross* contains at least a hint of this. After Carol's ski monologue, she exits the stage, and the maid enters. The stage directions describe her as a maternal figure: "holding two pillows, sheets, and bedspreads in her arms, she is rather fat and older than JIM . . . (103)." Yet there is a sexual dimension to the interaction between Jim and the maid from the outset. Jim is absorbed in adolescent male behavior doing push-ups; he invites her in to watch his "show" of masculinity ("come in, come in, have a bed or a seat or something," he says like a vaudevillian crowd puller):

Maid: I always seem to catch you at it don't I?
Jim: Yep. You catch me every time. I think you plan it.
Maid: No.
Jim: I think you do. You like catching me. (104)

The introductory exchange sparks with sexual innuendo: the maid's offhand greeting—implying that she catches Jim during his exercises everyday—also resonates with the implication that she has caught him in some sort of onanistic act, while Jim challenges the maid with the implication that she is sexually interested in his activities. The sexual implications of this exchange are extended when the maid attempts to change the bed and Jim attempts to stop her; here the maid takes on a maternal role and Jim an adolescent one:

Jim: Hey, leave my bed alone.
Maid: Well I have to change it dear.
Jim: Its got stains. I don't want you to see the stains. I get embarrassed. I do. It embarrasses me. I get pink and everything. (105)

Jim's embarrassment is that of the adolescent who fears his mother will discover the residues of his masturbation. The maid's maternal role is furthered not only by her advice to Jim to get his condition "taken care of," but by her interest in the procreation of crabs (one can envision her, during the following speech, cradling a pillow in her arms, with an expression of maternal interest animating her face):

> Maid: I'd have enough sense to have my bed changed, knowing that crabs lay eggs inside the sheets and blankets and that eggs hatch and that when eggs hatch new crabs are born and baby crabs grow up like all crabs have to. And when they're grown they lay new crabs and it goes on and on indefinitely like that for years (108).

If Jim inhabits a universe of embarrassment about "stains", the world of the father, the maid represents that maternal authority without guilt (her constant bed making is the symbolic equivalent of sphincteral training): she suggests that time in which body wastes were not seen as objects of embarrassment or shame ("I've seen yellow stains before, you know, they don't bother me"). Jim's evasive "bed changing" exercise in which he enlists the maid to shove beds around thus changing their places on stage is a kind of repression of guilt through physical activity; certainly it reveals the lengths to which he is prepared to go to hide the embarrassing stains. Thus beyond the Oedipal dynamics, the exchange sets up two realms: the maternal order versus the order of the phallus, and these two orders are involved in the nature of the competing dreams or fantasies of the two characters.

Jim as representative of the law of the father, ultimately the law of the symbolic order, is suggested in his presence as the only man on the stage, and in his ritualistic devotion to exercising. His fantasies are concerned with the phallic mastery of tree climbing ("all over the tree and clear up to the top"), swimming and jogging. Yet if the paternal world is that of the symbolic order (where paternal prohibitions institute symbolism, where the oral activity of the pre-verbal child is displaced from mother to speech), it is not attained without the paternal threat of castration. Thus Jim's genital crabs are associated with this threat. Jim explains to the maid that his genital crabs "pinch so hard I think they are going all the way through. They grab and squeeze. I think they must have teeth, too. Along with their pincers I think they have teeth" (108).

Here, as an overdetermined symbol, the crabs also take on the characteristics of the monstrous feminine—the horrifying sight of the mother's genitals which evokes castration anxiety in the male spectator condensed in the image of the vagina dentalia. Moreover, as an image of the abject associated with the "monstrous feminine" they suggest that simultaneous repulsion and fascination for the archaism of pre-oedipal relationships. This combination of sexual fascination and attraction for that undifferentiated "abject" state which signifies a collapse of distinctions and boundaries between self and not self, human and animal, is evoked when Jim questions the maid about medical assistance in the wilderness. Sexual innuendoes abound, and distinctions collapse between human doctors and veterinarians, medical treatment for humans and medical treatment for animals:

> There isn't one out here, huh? I mean they don't by any chance have a country doctor out in this neck of the woods. One a' them country guys in a model T Ford and a beat up leather bag full of sheep dip. Maybe even a veterinarian. I hear veterinarians can take as good care of you as a physician or real doctor. Have you heard that? (110)

The connection between this attraction to undifferentiation, and the preoedipal undifferentiated world of the mother is further underscored in Jim's fantasy of night swimming. Here clearly the return to the undifferentiated is associated with the return to the maternal. Jim's description of "night swimming in the middle of the forest" implies a descent into the preverbal and undifferentiated where mother and nature is synonymous, a return to the mother as originating womb, and a rebirth into preoedipal innocence:

> Your body stays warm inside. It's just the outside that gets wet. It's really neat. I mean you dive under water and hold your breath. You stay under for about five minutes. You stay down there and there's nothing but water all around you. Nothing but marine life. You stay down as long as you can until your lungs start to ache. They feel like they are going to burst open. Then just at the point where you can't stand it any more you force yourself to the top. You explode out of the water, gasping for air, and all this rain hits you in the face. You ought to try it. (115)

Yet the lure of the preoedipal maternal realm must be held at bay or repudiated by the subject of paternal law constructed in the symbolic order. This repudiation is accomplished, according to Kristeva, by the "ritual of defilement." As she puts it:

> This is precisely where we encounter the rituals of defilement
> and their derivatives, which, based on the feeling of abjection
> and all converging on the maternal, attempt to symbolize the
> threat to the subject: that of being swamped by the dual
> relationship, thereby risking the loss not of a part (castration)
> but of the totality of his living being. The function of these
> religious rituals is to ward off the subject's fear of his very own
> identity sinking irretrievably into the mother. (Kristeva, *Powers*
> 64)

This repudiation of the maternal is realized in the swimming lesson
which is such a central and arresting part of the play. If it is not exactly
a "ritual of defilement," it serves a similar function. If the maid
represents the maternal, then the swimming lesson, like the defilement
rite, serves to "ward off" the inviting maternal figure and the authority
she signifies, and to point to the boundary between maternal authority
and the paternal law of the phallus and the symbolic order. Here the
maid becomes the object of masculine orders, and the maternal body
subjected to the hyper-masculine discourse of a swimming coach whose
language is like a military drill sergeant: "Hup, Two. Hup,Two. Shake
it off. Use it! Keep using it so it doesn't tighten. Keep it loose! Hup,
two! Hup two!" (118). The ritualistic lesson, ironically conducted on
beds, in fact consists of the transformation of the libidinal body into a
machine. Jim instructs the maid to

> Regard your arms and legs as paddles. A paddle has a broad
> surface and reaches its highest point of thrust when it is
> perpendicular to the surface line of the water. This is the way
> you should use your arms. Keep your fingers close together to
> make a broader surface. Be careful not to let any water pass
> between them. That's it. Now the breathing is important. This
> requires added concentration and coordination. You will be able
> to breath instinctively and in the right manner if you keep in
> mind that the human being cannot inhale water. (117)

The maid protests her treatment as the object of this patriarchal
impulse to mastery ("I can't go plodding on like an Olympic champion
or something. Jesus Christ"), but Jim now occupies the dominant
position. Indeed Jim and the maid change places, and the maid now
assumes the characteristics of abjection. If menstrual blood is one of the

polluting entities in rituals of defilement, the maid's resulting "cramps" seem especially significant. Grovelling at Jim's feet the maid now assumes a variety of roles of the abject: the hysteric, the menstrual woman, the woman beset by Freud's "house-wife neurosis":

> So you don't like me screaming out here, is that it? You don't like me getting carried away with my cramps and my pain in the middle of the night in the middle of the forest. Well let me tell you it hurts me to do it. I don't like screaming myself. I try to keep a calm house, an easy home with everyone quiet and happy. Its not an easy thing, Jim. At my age and in my condition. (121–22)

With the maid now relegated "safely" to this abject position Jim assumes the masculine prerogative of mastery ("We can get you a doctor but you have to get up. Come on. I'll take you into town"). Yet Shepard's world of competing fantasies is extraordinarily unstable, and discursive and ideological positionings precarious and changeable. If Jim's mock swimming lesson has assigned the maid to her "proper" position, subjected to the law of the phallus, she will not remain the subject of patriarchal ideology. In her "competing fantasy" she creates a world associated with the generative, procreative, undifferentiated maternal principle, outside the paternal function of naming, establishing meaning and signification, and positing an "I" that is stable. The maid's fantasy is about the death of the subject into the watery world of the mermaid, preoedipal "phallic" mother no longer bound by the matrix of the family, nor confined by patriarchal ideology and the fixed identity necessitated by entry into symbolic order.

> But once its over it isn't so bad at all. Once you get over the shock of having water all around and dragonflies and water lilies floating by and little silver fish flashing around you. Once that's past and you get all used to your flippers and your fins and your new skin, then it comes very easy . . . You move through the water like you were born in that very same place and never even knew what land was like. You dive and float and sometimes rest on the bank and maybe chew on some watercress. And that family in town forgets who you are and you forget all about swimming lessons and just swim without knowing how. . . . (122–23)

The maid's speech is such a stunning turn in the play direction because it undercuts Jim's masculine, "thetic" world of organizing experience discursively, of naming and instruction-giving, of struggle and mastery ("You can't poop out in the middle of the lake"), and transforms it into a maternal underwater world, a preverbal world of instinctual drives where the jouissance of death and rebirth is coextensive with nature and seasonal change:

> . . . and before you know it the winter has come and the lake has frozen and you sit on the bank staring at the ice. You don't move at all. You just sit very still staring at the ice until you don't feel a thing. Until your flippers freeze to the ground and your tail freezes to the grass and you stay like that for a very long time until summer comes around. (123)

This imaginative world is connected with the instinctual semioticizing body that is heterogeneous to signification, as opposed to the world of symbolic legislation that is based on the prohibition of incest and represented by the father. As such the maid's phantasy is one of the most "poetic" moments in the play, and constitutes an allegory of the poetic process itself which is remarkably Kristevian: the maternal semiotic "breaks through" the paternal symbolic, subverting the repressive mastery of discourse (and of the body/text) suggested by Jim's military orders. More than that, the maid's vision overturns the very notion of the maternal as abject, a construction of the paternal symbolic order which functions to protect the integrity of that order. The pull of the undifferentiated/maternal, rather than something to be constructed as the monstrous feminine or as abject, something to be guarded against or expelled, is privileged, and we are left with a powerful image of the oceanic mother whose generative and procreative principles lie outside patriarchal constructs and outside the law.

This moment of "inversion" poses a radical threat to the stability of the symbolic order, signifying all that which is untenable in the symbolic, paternal function which through prohibition and differentiation produces meaning. It is also directly related to that final overdetermined image in the play—revealed when Jim, back to audience, staring (longingly?) after the departed maid, turns to expose the stream of blood running down his forehead. In *Desire in Language* Kristeva speaks of the paternal function as a "sacrificial function," insofar as symbolic and social cohesion are maintained by a kind of sacrifice "which makes of a *soma* a sign towards an unnameable transcendence . . ." (Kristeva, 138). Jim's wound might then be construed as a sign of sacrifice, a mark of the price paid for renouncing the maternal world to enter the paternal symbolic order. For it suggests an upwardly displaced image of castration, the result of discovering sexual difference, where the mother's *pas-de-phallus* produces castration anxiety, and where the law of the father is maintained by the threat of emasculation. As a wound it signifies loss and destruction, the fact that the symbolic function is maintained at the cost of repressing instinctual drives and the desire for the lost mother. Freud invoked Schelling's dictum that everything is uncanny "that ought to have remained hidden and secret and yet comes to light" (Stertz 301), and in this sense the final image of the play is decidedly uncanny: like Oedipus's gouged-out eye it acknowledges at once the strength of incestuous desire and the necessity for its renunciation in order to maintain signifying and social structures. The stream of blood running down Jim's forehead is also another image of the abject itself. Its resemblance to a "red cross" again suggests the sacrificial dimension of the wound, but as something abject it represents the risk to which the symbolic order is permanently exposed by the undifferentiated and "unclean," by that which simultaneously threatens and defines; indeed its affinity to the shape of a cross suggests the close connection between abjection and the sacred, the pervious boundary between the sacred and sacrificial and the horrific and abominable, and hence the fragility of the law of the symbolic order.

Thus the final image not only underscores the instability of the symbolic order, but again highlights the loss involved in a process of signification based on prohibition of incest and "thetic" signification based on paternal law. The bloodied forehead recalls Kristeva's description of the abject as "the violence of mourning for an object that has always already been lost" (*Powers* 15). More than this it suggests, again like Oedipus' wound, the problematic relation between desire and language at the heart of Shepard's play: that entry into language inaugurates desire, and restless desire finds no final satisfaction in language. Again to quote Kristeva, "the gouged out eye, the wound [signifies] the basic incompleteness that conditions the indefinite quest of the signifying concatenations" (*Powers* 89).

References

Bloom, Michael. "Visions of the End: The Early Plays," in *American Dreams: The Imagination of Sam Shepard*. Ed. Bonnie Marranca. New York: PAJ Publications, 1981.

Creed, Barbara. "Horror and the Monstrous Feminine: An Imaginary Abjection," *Screen* 27.7 (1986): 44–70.

Freud, Sigmund. *The Interpretation of Dreams* in *The Basic Writings of Sigmund Freud*. Ed. A.A. Brill. New York: Random House, 1938.

Hertz, Neil. "Freud and the Sandman," in *Textual Strategies: Perspectives in Post Structuralist Criticism*. Ed. Josue V. Harari. Ithaca: Cornell, 1979.

Kristeva, Julia. *Desire in Language: A Semiotic Approach to Literature and Art*. Ed. Leon S. Roudiez. New York: Columbia, 1980.

———. *Powers of Horror: An Essay on Abjection*. Ed. Leon S. Roudiez. New York: Columbia, 1982.

Shepard, Sam. *Chicago and Other Plays*. New York: Urizen, 1967.

Wilcox, Leonard. "Modernism and Post Modernism: *Tooth of the Crime* and the Discourses of Popular Culture," *Modern Drama*, 30.4 (1987).

ADAPTING TO REALITY: LANGUAGE IN SHEPARD'S *CURSE OF THE STARVING CLASS*

Phyllis R. Randall

Thus far the critics cannot agree whether Sam Shepard's best play is *True West* or *Buried Child* or *Curse of the Starving Class* or *A Lie of the Mind*. They cannot agree whether the major influence on his writing has been movies or drugs or the off-Off-Broadway movement of the sixties or music, and, if music, whether rock or country and western. But there is one aspect about his plays that all agree on—his remarkable language. The impact and the range of Shepard's language are noted by just about everybody who writes about him. D.J.R. Bruckner in the *New York Times* tells of Shepard's "bursts of lyric fever" that result in a language "almost Elizabethan in its richness, variety and detail" (sec. H:3). Richard Gilman writes of his "marvelous ear, not for actual speech but for the imagined possibilities of utterances as invention, as victory over silence" (xxi). Schechner says that Shepard's plays are "words, and sounds, and the lost American idioms" (697). No one fails to notice the virtuosity of the idioms that Shepard has mastered. Marranca writes of his plays being identifiable "by their highly individualized use of American vernacular speech." She notes his "wonderful ear for the different rhythms of speech," including "cowboy talk, hipster argot, rock rhythms, contemporary slang, and language

from the worlds of science fiction, gangsters, and sports" (81). Herbert
Blau extends the list: "The language can be dazzling, since Shepard has
a fantastic ear for all the subcultural vernaculars of American life and
the polyglottism of regional speech: blacks, gays, rockers, rappers, jazz
sidemen and Rotary Clubbers, drifters, gangsters, Holy Rollers, drug
freaks and rodeo riders, the New Wave and the Old Frontier, the voice of
the urban cowboy and . . . the lumpen voice of the rural suburbs"
(524).

Such fecundity of dialect and voices conforms well with both the
tone and the content of Shepard's early plays, those "collages," as Cohn
calls them, "in which the characters talk past one another," and those
plays that include "fantastic or mythological characters" (*Essays* 161)
who change identities at will. But what happens to all these
extravagances of language in Shepard's later plays, the ones Cohn
classifies as realistic (*Essays* 161)? Of the realistic plays, *Curse of the
Starving Class, Buried Child,* and *True West* (Shepard has called them
his "family trilogy" [Cohn, *New American* 183]), it is the first that I
shall concentrate on here. Perhaps because it was the first of these
family dramas to be written (staged in London in 1977, in New York
the following year [King 198]), *Curse of the Starving Class* retains
many of the features of language which we do not ordinarily associate
with realistic drama. How Shepard has molded these features anew is the
subject of this investigation.

In the early plays, characters frequently adopt several voices to find
which one is theirs, to discover who they are, much like an actor
working out a role, as Blau has pointed out (525). Perhaps the most
brilliant example of this voice-adoption technique is in Shepard's play
with music, *The Tooth of Crime,* where a verbal duel is fought using
all the different voices the combatants, Hoss and Crow, can assume
without "losing their cool." The trick of each is not only to invent new
voices but also to adapt to the style, the lingo, that the other assumes
without any indication that he himself has been forced to adapt.

To use that technique again in *Curse,* Shepard must find more
natural reasons to have his characters speak in more than one voice.
Weston, for example, is a drunken ne'er-do-well, negligent of his land
and family, who, at the miracle of the filled refrigerator, becomes
converted, a new person. In this age of publicity about born-again
Christians, nothing could be more a part of ordinary existence. Before
the conversion, he rants, raves, and bellows. Much of his early dialogue

is printed in capital letters. After the conversion, however, he is shown to be introspective. Before the conversion his language is vulgar, curt, lower-class colloquial: the desert land he bought turned out to be "A real piece of shit" (Shepard, *Curse of the Starving Class* 159). To care for the maggoty lamb, he advises Wesley to "Put some a' that blue shit on it. That'll fix him up" (160). After the conversion, cleansed in body, reclothed, his language becomes middle-class standard in both content and style, suitable for broadcast into homes all over America: "I finished the new door. Did you notice?. . . This could be a great place if somebody'd take some interest in it" (185).

Weston is not the only character with a reason for speaking in different voices. Emma, the daughter, is also in search of a true self. She is an adolescent, just experiencing her first menstruation—"she's got the curse," her mother explains to her brother (156). This adolescent has typically mercurial shifts in mood, as well as wild swings between being adult and child. And so Shepard can make Emma by turns wise— she sees that her mother is really looking for self-esteem—and foolish—she behaves impetuously. This behavior leads to her being dragged through the mud by a wild horse (Act I), to her being jailed after a shooting spree at the Alibi Club (Act II), and finally to her being blown to bits in the Kaiser-Fraser, the car booby-trapped for her father (Act III). In her adult voice Emma can carry on a mature conversation with her mother about the futility of their going to Europe. Ella seems to think that just getting away will solve all their problems; Emma can see that they will carry their problems with them wherever they go: "It'd be the same as here[;] . . . we'd all be the same people" (148).

But she can also be the conventionally bratty adolescent meeting an outsider, giving him the once-over, finally deciding, to his face, that lawyer Taylor is "creepy" and "weird" (151). She is the straight-A student who works hard at her 4-H project, yet fantasizes about becoming a car mechanic in Mexico—or, later, a criminal: "I'm going into crime. It's the only thing that pays these days" (197).

Indeed, these wide shifts in the language behavior of Weston and Emma are so "natural" that the extreme behavior of the one-dimensional gangsters at the end of the play strikes a resoundingly false note, as Marranca has observed (107). The gangsters Slater and Emerson seem like walk-ons from an earlier play, perhaps *Mad Dog Blues*. They seem to be imitating Peter Lorre at his most grotesquely sinister—the butchered lamb carcass "Looks like somebody's afterbirth" (199), Slater says as they laugh hysterically. Such lines remind us of the truth of Richard Schechner's observation years before Shepard wrote this play that the source of his language is not the street but "the recording studio, the movies, and late night TV" (698). That is, the dialogue sounds like what the media have established as the language of the streets, an imitation of dialogue imitating life.

Being able to use different voices in a natural way is one of Shepard's triumphs of transferring the language devices of the earlier plays into this realistic play. Another triumph derives from his paying attention, especially in *Curse of the Starving Class*, to the use of language as conversation, that is, to the use of dialogue to seem like conversation, following the norms of conversation that audiences anticipate (which, of course, are not exactly the norms that conversational analysts have been uncovering. See Robert Cohen for some of these differences). The earlier plays, plays in which, for example, Jesse James and Mae West ride off together on Paul Bunyan's ox, just do not call for the same kind of conversational style as plays in which a family is about to lose its farm.

Shepard is certainly aware of conversation as a topic, of writing it, and of what its conventional rules must be. In *Buried Child*, Shelly, returning with boyfriend Vince to visit with his grandparents, becomes more at home than Vince and fits into the family better. Winning over Vince's dim-witted father, Tilden, apparently because she is willing to sit down and peel carrots, she says to Tilden that they might have a conversation.

> We can?
> > Sure. We're having a conversation right now.
> We are?
> > Yes. That's what we're doing. (101)

That is what conversation is—each one saying something relevant to the other, taking turns, making sense, even when the conversation itself is on a topic abundantly forgettable and banal.

In *Curse of the Starving Class*, Shepard is not so open in talking about what conversation is, but in the beginning of the play he highlights, even emphasizes, some of the norms of conversation. He does so, it seems to me, in order to make a sharp contrast with the less-than-logical, other-than-normal conversation which is to follow. The play begins in the most traditional of all ways; indeed the opening scene would have served Ibsen well. The characters talk over the events of the night before. The conversation is informative, logical, and "normal"; it follows all of the norms of ordinary conversation. Remarks are pertinent to the situation (cleaning up the debris of a broken door), answers are relevant to the questions, and both of the participants, the mother, Ella, and the son, Wesley, take turns in the conversation freely, with no evasions or hidden agendas. In fact, Shepard's dialogue stresses how logically the two characters think: Ella called the police because she thought her life was threatened. After all, the intruder, if truly her husband, Weston, could have entered the house in other ways besides breaking down the door. Also speaking logically, Wesley chides her with locking the door; the normal way for somebody who lived in the house to get in would be through the door. Wesley guesses that his father must have taken the Packard to get away; Ella responds that if that is the car that is missing, then that is the one he took. Elementary deduction. Logic at its easiest.

All of this stress on logic establishes a norm and gives us the sense that we are in a situation that we can understand in our usual ways. No sooner is it established, however, than the norm is broken. Wesley begins a long reverie about the previous night. The soliloquy, standard fare in the earlier plays where it is just one more surrealistic element, certainly breaks the continuity of the realism. Surely, then, the mold is broken for a reason. This soliloquy seems to serve as a Brechtian device, that is, a conscious device to subvert our complacency about what is normal, our sense of comfortableness with the Ibsen-like exposition that we have been hearing. (Cohn notes a Brechtian influence in Shepard's use of music in *Tooth of Crime* [*Essays* 167].) It is worth looking more closely at this soliloquy and the new reality it introduces.

Wesley's reverie is a soliloquy of the young man as artist, vividly aware of what is going on inside himself as he hears his father coming home drunk, breaking down the door, yelling at his mother, and finally leaving in the Packard. During the reverie, the actors are instructed by Shepard to continue their business: Wesley continues to load the wheelbarrow with the debris from the door and Ella continues to fix some breakfast. So the monologue is not a freeze-frame device, although certainly something of Shepard's work in motion pictures has been carried over into his playwriting techniques (see Carroll). Wesley's reverie provides the audience with some reflection time too. The few lines of dialogue thus far have already established major themes, tensions, and conflicts of this play. Wesley and Ella have each referred to not knowing another's identity. Ella has indicated that she was not sure who was breaking down the door, though she acknowledges that she could smell the intruder through the door, specifically the smell, not of alcohol, but of his skin. Since smell is one of the more intimate ways of knowing another, we are made aware of the idea of the stranger living in our midst, of his (and our own) unknowableness even within the family. Wesley, too, has commented on an unfamiliar identity. Calling the police, he tells his mother, was more than humiliating. It "Makes me feel like we're someone else" (137). Just a few lines later, however, when he begins his reverie, he reports totally subjective sensations that can have meaning only through a consciousness, a mind aware of itself experiencing. He smells the avocado blossoms, hears the coyotes, feels himself in bed, sees the model airplanes hanging above him, suspended from the ceiling. The planes excite his imagination; now he becomes the enemy, floating in the "black" space of the world while the planes search for him. He becomes like an animal, listening intently. With sharpened acuity he hears the Packard as his father comes home from his bout of drinking. Now the imagined details intertwine with reality—he "sees" his father sitting in the car, tucking a bottle of Tiger Rose under his arm, and he hears the altercation of the previous night: "Foot kicking door. Man's voice. Dad's voice. Dad calling Mom. No answer. Foot kicking. Foot kicking harder. Wood splitting. Man's voice. In the night" (138). This concentrated, rhythmic language, highly charged with sensory images of every sort, establishes Wesley as a budding poet, a creative sensibility. The soliloquy is a portrait in miniature of the artist as a young man.

This lyrical reverie, of course, is a retelling of the previous night's dreary domestic fight, a welding of poetic process to prosaic subject matter as startling in its way as any of the linguistic devices of the earlier plays. Nor is it the only startling juxtaposition of incongruities in this scene. All during the reverie the audience is acutely aware of what Ella is doing, for she is frying bacon, surely one of the homeliest pieces of stage business that Shepard could have invented. If we can call the smell of frying bacon lyrical, then the scene before us reinforces, echoes, the kind of welding found in Wesley's reverie. For while we are caught up in the olfactory lyricism of frying bacon, we are put off by the visual reality. The bacon is being fried by a bathrobed, hair-in-curlers, frumpy housewife, working in a dirty, debris-filled kitchen.

This kind of dichotomy and many other instances of echoing permeate the play. The point here, however, is that by the end of the reverie we are prepared to face a new reality. Shepard signals it in two ways. When Wesley leaves with the wheelbarrow load of splintered wood, this potential artist, this reveller in lyric language, like a child mimics the sound of a car speeding off. Shepard signals the shift in reality through Ella, too. She begins to talk, to carry on what appears to be normal discourse—except that she is now alone on stage. Moreover, the topic she brings up has no reference to anything that has preceded it. The basic rules of conversation have been broken; our sense of order and logic is violated. The daughter, Emma, enters, carrying her how-to-cut-up-a-chicken charts, and picks up on her mother's statements as if this is indeed a normal conversation. The topic turns out to be Emma's first menstrual period, a topic which shatters the conventions of the stage just as what is said shatters our expectations of logic. Ella wants Emma to know the "facts," but Emma would be better off if she picked up her information elsewhere, so wrong is Ella. The humor of the scene comes from Ella's pigheadedness: swimming draws out the blood; coins carry germs, so coin-operated sanitary pad dispensers are forbidden. It is a relief to laugh, since our sense of order and logic and what is normal is upset.

Moreover, it will continue to be upset. Ella, the mother, has eaten the chicken Emma needs for her 4-H demonstration project. A mother eating something her child needs? Ella tries to inject some old-fashioned logic into the situation: when Emma accuses her of using the chicken for soup or something, Ella retorts, "Why would I use a fryer for soup" (140). (Implied, of course, is that one uses a stewing hen for soup.) When Wesley returns, he too is a different person. Continuing with a new version of logical conversation, he asks if the chicken had Emma's name on it, and since, literally, it did not, he declares that she has nothing to be screaming about. Whether in retaliation for her outcry or as a next "logical" step to show his contempt for anyone who tries to chart "just bones," he urinates on Emma's charts.

Here again we have a scene involving many senses. Emma is outside yelling, getting rid of her anger over her mother's eating the chicken. Meanwhile, her mother sits, unperturbed, breakfasting alone in front of her children, although she has already categorized the family as belonging to the starving class. (No wonder Emma turns the tables on the usual line and calls her mother a spoiled brat.) All the while the brother is urinating on Emma's charts. By now a drunken father breaking down the door to get in his own house seems not only understandable behavior but "normal" compared to the behavior of these other members of the family. "What kind of family is this?" Emma asks as she reenters the kitchen, voicing our concern as well (142).

It is the kind of family where the mother lies (she tells Emma that she tried to stop Wesley) and schemes (she plans to sell the house without her husband's knowledge) and undoubtedly commits adultery (the lunch meeting with her lawyer lasts overnight). But, because of her contradictory nature, Ella, too, can speak as two persons, although her style of speaking does not change. Sometimes she is the concerned mother looking out for her children; other times she is the selfish woman embittered by all she has missed in life. At one moment she is concerned about the danger to Emma in taking the wild horse, and the next she is complacent about it since she does not want to bother herself to go look. One moment she can speak logically about the arrangements she has made with the lawyer to sell the house without her husband's signature, and the next, when challenged, she has to fall back on the jargon of a real estate broker to defend herself: "It's the only sure investment. It can never depreciate like a car or a washing machine. Land will double its value in ten years. In less than that. Land is going up every day" (146). In relying on this safe patter, Ella is obviously echoing what she has learned from Taylor, the man handling the deal for her, since he himself also resorts to this kind of safe patter when embarrassed (when Emma brings up the topic of his intimate knowledge of her mother—"Does she bleed?" [153]) or threatened (when Wesley points out that Taylor is the same man who sold his father worthless land in the desert some years before [179]).

Ella's speaking in two voices is, again, realistic. It reflects the dual nature of her character. On the other hand, it is much less dramatic than the dual voices of Weston as sinner and saint, or of Emma as child and adult, or of Wesley as artist-in-reverie and son-losing-his-identity. It is the wider swings, particularly of the two men, which allow scope for richness of language and for using some of the language techniques honed in the earlier plays. This richer language undoubtedly helps give the impression that the two male characters are more fully realized than the two female characters. Shepard's difficulty with creating fully realized female characters has been noted by others (see, for example, Marranca 84, 103; Blau 521; and Auerbach in this collection).

One of those richer language techniques I have already mentioned, the soliloquy. Cohn, who calls Shepard's striking use of the soliloquy his trademark (*Essays* 170), comments on their "Inventive, associative . . . image-laden" qualities (*New American* 174). Schechner notes that these speeches, "not unlike the Elizabethan monolog-soliloquy," are designed as "probes, continuums, searches for identification and verification" (698). Since these probes are almost always concerned with self-awareness, Blau labels them "Whitmanian flecks and flashes of a performing self, the body leaping through a sluice of disjunct images to some other dimension, going with the flux of words, a long jazz-riff of images reaching toward an identity" (524).

The only such "Whitmanian" soliloquy in *Curse of the Starving Class* is Wesley's reverie, which, as I noted earlier, might be labeled a Brechtian device since it signals that the logical norm established up to that point has been illusion and that a new kind of reality is about to jostle our complacency about what is normal, what is real. But there are other and very different solo pieces in the play, and they deserve a look as well. Unlike a soliloquy, these solo pieces do not stop the forward motion of the play, but are a part of it. Yet each is far longer than a normal conversational turn; hence my term, "solo."

Weston frequently talks to himself in the guise of addressing whatever is nearby, generally the lamb. These solos, however, are totally unlike Wesley's. Weston talks to himself about what is happening or what is going through his mind about his surroundings— no introspection, no reverie. In fact, his solos are, as Weston himself acknowledges, conversations with himself. Since he is so isolated from his family, he has taken to talking to himself: "Always was best at talkin' to myself. Always was the best thing. Nothing like it. Keeps ya' company at least" (192). So he can talk to the lamb, asking why it is in the kitchen, and express his indignation at the sight of the empty refrigerator. "WE'VE DONE IT AGAIN! WE'VE GONE AND LEFT EVERYTHING UP TO THE OLD MAN AGAIN! ALL THE UPKEEP! THE MAINTENANCE! PERFECT!" (157). Of course, we already know that Weston has done little about upkeep and maintenance and keeping the refrigerator filled, so we hear these rantings "logically," that is, as the rantings of an unkempt drunk, an inept farmer, a failed husband and father.

Parallel to this scene in Act I is the one at the beginning of Act III, after the conversion. Again Weston is alone in the kitchen with the lamb, but this time he is expansive in his solo. He begins by addressing the lamb, which he has treated for maggots, and then tells him a story, the one of an eagle coming to pick up the lamb testicles that Weston had thrown up on the roof of a shed for an eagle. The story is part and parcel of Weston's rejuvenation; he sits in the cleaned-up kitchen, bathed, shaved, and freshly clothed, folding the clothes he has washed for the others in the family, and recounts a tale that exhilarates him, that reminds him of feelings he has not had since World War II days when he first went up in a B-29. The reference to the airplane, of course, echoes the references to the airplanes in Wesley's reverie in Act I, and is just one more indication of the important father-son identity theme in the play. At this point, Weston is more like the young Wesley, full of remembered feelings and sensations. In turn, Wesley, when he enters at the end of the solo, will try to follow his father's program for rejuvenation (a hot bath followed by a cold one followed by a naked walk around the farm) and finds instead that he becomes, not rejuvenated, but his unconverted father.

Weston has one other brief solo in Act III, after he has fixed breakfast for Wesley, who has wandered off. (The situation and the odor of frying ham and eggs echo the opening scene in Act I, when Ella was frying bacon.) Ella lies asleep on the table (just as Weston himself had done earlier). So Weston converses with himself, wondering why Wesley carried the lamb out, wondering if he should go ahead and eat this breakfast since it will only get cold (he does, an echo of Ella's behavior earlier). In other words, he is still, despite his conversion, enough of the old Weston to find conversation with himself better than silence. And so, despite the conversion, when he finds that the hit men are after him, he takes his usual way out of a dilemma—he runs off.

Emma, like her mother always making plans, also has two longish talks, one alone and one a part of a conversation. They contrast with Wesley's soliloquy in a number of ways. The one alone is an address to the empty refrigerator, humorous but hardly lyrical: "Any corn muffins in there? Hello! Any produce? Any rutabagas? Any root vegetables?" (150). This Pinter technique of piling on incongruous images works for humor but hardly for character, and so it seems to me a false or derivative note. More in keeping with her established style is Emma's long speech to Wesley at the beginning of Act II when they are sitting together in the kitchen, she working on a new chart to replace the one Wesley urinated on, and he making a new back door, while artichokes boil on the stove. ("Smells like stale piss," Ellis will comment when he enters [175], an olfactory echo of Act I.) Emma makes up a story about her mother and lawyer Taylor in Mexico having car trouble in a town where she herself is the mechanic. Unrecognized, she solves all their mechanical problems and, through dirty tricks, makes a bundle of money in the bargain. Though it reveals Emma as imaginative story teller, the tale is of a totally different sort both from Wesley's reverie and from Weston's eagle story. Both men stress feelings and sensations; Emma stresses narrative. The language is different, too: Emma speaks in complete sentences, full of detail, but totally devoid of consciousness of self. "But they break down somewhere outside a little place called Los Cerritos. They have to hike five miles to town. They come to a small beat-up gas station with one pump and a dog with three legs" (162). By contrast, Weston speaking to the lamb about the eagle says, "Well, I was working away out there when I felt this shadow across me. . . . Felt like the way it does when the clouds move across the sun. Huge and black and cold like. . . . I could hear his sound real clear. A giant bird. His wings made a kind of crackling noise" (184). The parallels between this language and that of Wesley's reverie are evident, not only establishing their link but also the difference of both from Emma's more prosaic language.

Emma's made-up fantasy solo about being a car mechanic in Mexico also contrasts sharply with Wesley's solo just a few minutes later when he is trying to impress on her the seriousness of their situation. He, too, is imagining a scenario, just as Emma had, but he tells it with far more attention to style than to narrative, to language rather than to events. "There'll be bulldozers crashing through the orchard. There'll be giant steel balls crashing through the walls. There'll be foremen with their sleeves rolled up and blueprints under their arms. There'll be steel girders spanning acres of land. Cement pilings. Prefab walls. Zombie architecture, owned by invisible zombies, built by zombies for the use and convenience of other zombies. A zombie city!" (164). This is language of a very different sort, and renews our impression of Wesley as a potential artist.

Only one of the long speeches in *Curse of the Starving Class*, then, is much like Shepard's typical, earlier soliloquies. Wesley's soliloquy/reverie gives us our sense of him as a potential artist; we hear it echoed once in his father's story after Weston's conversion. In general, however, Wesley's lyric style, whether in a soliloquy/reverie or in a story-telling solo contrasts with the story-telling styles of his unconverted father and his sister. The lyric style contrasts as well with the language of the last story, a story Wesley himself takes part in telling.

The play ends with the completion of the eagle story, told jointly by Ella and Wesley, who by now has assumed the identity of his father. Wesley has, in effect, been "unconverted," a sign that the curse in the family has been handed down intact. The effect of the curse shows in the language. Gone are the vivid images, the piling-on of sensations. Gone is any introspection. The story is told as straightforward fact, with no embellishments. "And that eagle comes down and picks up the cat in his talons and carries him screaming off into the sky," says Wesley. "That's right," responds his mother. Wesley continues, "And the eagle's being torn apart in midair. The eagle is trying to free himself from the cat, and the cat won't let go." "And they come crashing down to the earth," his mother finishes (201).

Wesley has not only changed his clothes; he has changed his language as well. The shift in the style of story telling signals his destruction, his fate, his inheritance from his father, just as clearly as his shift in clothes. Marranca has written that Wesley is the only one in the family who survives the emotional devastation at the end of the play (107). Surely not. The Wesley of the beginning of the play, the potential artist, has been blown into as many pieces as the car that contains his sister, Emma.

Concentrating on Shepard's use of language in *Curse of the Starving Class*, I have barely touched on the many themes of the play, and I have certainly not examined all its strengths. I have tried to show that Shepard could continue to use some of the surrealistic linguistic devices of his plays of the 1960s and the early 1970s in this realistic play of 1977 and use them to good effect. In a statement written for *Performing Arts Journal*, Shepard noted his continuing interest in the idea of consciousness. It follows, then, that his version of the realistic will be more concerned with interior reality than with exterior reality. In language terms, that means with the reality of thoughts and the thought processes, not with the outer rules and conventions of conversation, as he teaches us in the opening scene of this play. That *Performing Arts Journal* statement, published in 1977, the same year that *Curse of the Starving Class* opened in London, goes on: "For some time now it's become generally accepted that the other art forms are dealing with this idea [of consciousness] to one degree or another. That the subject of painting is seeing. That the subject of music is hearing. That the subject of sculpture is space. But what is the subject of theatre which includes all of these and more?" (14). Whatever else it is, the subject of theater is language. An examination of Sam Shepard's language would, therefore, seem to be a good place to ground an understanding of his plays.

References

Blau, Herbert. "The American Dream in American Gothic: The Plays of Sam Shepard and Adrienne Kennedy," *Modern Drama* 27 (1984): 520–39.

Bruckner, D.J.R. "Forging a New Dramatic Language," *New York Times,* 7 July 1985, sec. H:1, 3.

Carroll, Dennis. "The Filmic Cut and 'Switchback' in the Plays of Sam Shepard," *Modern Drama* 28 (1985): 125–38.

Cohen, Robert. "Spoken Dialogue in Written Drama," *Essays in Theatre* 4 (1986): 85–97.

Cohn, Ruby. "Sam Shepard: Today's Passionate Shepard and His Loves." *Essays on Contemporary American Drama.* Ed. Hedwig Bock and Albert Wertheim. Munich: Hueber Verlag, 1981, 161–72.

———. "The Word is My Shepard." *New American Dramatists, 1960-1980.* New York: Grove Press, 1982, 171–86.

Gilman, Richard. Introduction. *Sam Shepard: Seven Plays.* New York: Bantam Books, 1981, ix–xxv.

King, Kimball. "Sam Shepard," *Ten Modern American Playwrights: An Annotated Bibliography.* New York: Garland, 1982, 197–213.

Marranca, Bonnie. "Sam Shepard," *American Playwrights: A Critical Survey.* Vol. 1. Ed. Bonnie Marranca and Gautam Dasgupta. New York: Drama Book Specialists, 1981, 81–111.

Schechner, Richard. "Sam Shepard." *Contemporary Dramatists.* Ed. James Vinson. New York: St. Martin's Press, 1973, 696–99.

Shepard, Sam. "American Experimental Theatre: Then and Now," *Performing Arts Journal* 2, No. 2 (Fall 1977): 13–14.

———. *Buried Child. Seven Plays.* New York: Bantam Books, 1981, 61–132.

————. *Curse of the Starving Class. Seven Plays.* New York: Bantam Books, 1981, 133–201.

GREAT EXPECTATIONS: LANGUAGE AND THE PROBLEM OF PRESENCE IN SAM SHEPARD'S WRITING

Ann Wilson

Walt Whitman was a great man. He expected something from America. He had this great expectation.

—Sam Shepard, *Action*

Sam Shepard is the pre-eminent playwright of the contemporary American theatre. His work has received numerous awards including the Pulitzer Prize in 1979 for *Buried Child*. Despite his success, Shepard has not always felt comfortable identifying himself as a writer. In the program note to *Cowboy Mouth*, the play which he co-wrote with Patti Smith, he announced, "I don't want to be a playwright, I want to be a rock and roll star" (Shewey 81). Later in the same note, he claims that "writing is neat because you do it on a physical level. Just like rock and roll" (Shewey 81). As glib as these two remarks may seem at first, they do suggest reasons for Shepard's ambivalence about writing.

The writer's medium is language which Shepard believes "has become so corrupt, laundered, stripped of meaning. We often don't know what we mean anymore" (Wren 90). In forging the link between writing and music, particularly jazz and rock-and-roll—two modes of music which often involve improvisation, Shepard expresses his yearning for a pure language which does not mediate experience but acts as a transparent medium which reveals fully the signified. He wants to discover a language in which the signifier does not *re*present the signified but makes it present. It is this sense of language which allows Michael Earley to suggest that Shepard is heir to the transcendentalist tradition of American writing because he "brings to the drama a liberating interplay of word, theme and image that has always been the hallmark of romantic writing" (127). While I agree with Earley that there is a strain in Shepard's writing which relates his work to that of the transcendentalist poets (especially Whitman), it is misleading to suggest that this is a strictly literary influence. The desire to discover a language or mode of representation which makes fully present the signifier is evident in a number of American cultural projects including the work of Shepard's friend and sometime collaborator, Joseph Chaikin and music (particularly jazz and rock and roll).

In an essay called "Language, Visualization and the Inner Library," he writes,

> From time to time I've practiced Jack Kerouac's discovery of jazz-sketching with words. Following the exact same principles as a musician does when he's jamming. After periods of this kind of practice, I begin to get the haunting sense that something in me writes but it's not necessarily me. At least it's not the "me" that takes credit for it. This identical experience happened to me once when I was playing drums with the Holy Modal Rounders, and it scared the shit out of me. Peter Stampfel, the fiddle player, explained it as being visited by the Holy Ghost, which sounded reasonable enough at the time. (205)

Shepard's remarks suggest that he constructs writing as a mysterious process which requires inspiration and which, when truly executed, has the power to reveal the unknown. He said, "I feel a lot of reluctance in attempting to describe any part of a process which, by its truest nature, holds unending mystery" (214). In answer to Amy Lippman's question about why he writes, Shepard responded, "I try to go into parts of myself that are unknown. And I think that those parts are related to everybody. They are not unique to me. They're not my personal domain" (21). From such a perspective the writer records his privileged vision; yet, necessarily, the rendering of the vision is always distorted and imperfect. "Words, at best, can only give a partial glimpse into the total world of sensate experience" (Shepard, 216). Despite his recognition of the limitations of language, Shepard still believes in the unrealized ideal of a language which can represent fully.

Although his remark about the inspiration of the Holy Ghost seems off-hand, it indicates his sense of the essential mystery of writing. If we remember that "inspiration" is from the Latin words *in* and *spirare*, then the writer who has been inspired (or "visited") by the Holy Ghost is one into whom the Holy Ghost has breathed. The entry of the Holy Ghost into the body of the writer is a moment of unity when the spirit and body are one and utterance is pure because the signifier (spirit) and the signified (the sign) are one. Within a religious context, the unification of thought and expression which is said to create a pure, unmediated language, is called glossolalia. This is not to suggest that Shepard's theatre is evangelical but rather that his sense of language gives it a theological impulse. He admires Shakespeare because his language authentically represents the human condition. He "traveled very far in himself to find it. The language didn't come out of the air, it came from a tremendous search, a religious experience" (Wren 81).

Shepard seeks to discover within himself the language which will make the signified fully present by overcoming loss which attends the separation of the signifier and the signified. Jacques Derrida in his essay "Theater of Cruelty" calls this language "glossopoeia."

> Glossopoeia, which is neither an imitative language nor a creation of names, takes us back to the borderline of the moment when the word has not yet been born, when articulation is no longer a shout but not yet discourse, when repetition is *almost* impossible, and along with it language in general: the separation of concept and sound, of the signified from signifier, of the pneumatical and the grammatical, the freedom of translation and tradition, the movement of interpretation, the difference between the soul and the body, the master and the slave, God and man, author and actor. (240)

Derrida suggests that the failure of the project is inscribed at the moment of inception when he writes "repetition is *almost* impossible." As indicated, emphasis falls on "almost" because if glossopoeia is a language, albeit one which is liminal, then there must be the possibility of its repetition because this is the defining characteristic of language. Thus, the originary moment of language when the signified is made fully present by the signifier is always elusive, approached but never reached.

This sense of the failure of language to reveal fully that which it signifies marks the particularly American quality of Shepard's writing. Harold Bloom suggests, "Emerson wanted Freedom, reconciled himself to Fate, but loved only Power, from first to last and I believe this to be true also of the central line of American poets coming after him" (*Poems* 8). He explains that Emerson defines the terms "Freedom," "Fate," and "Power" as follows:

> Freedom or "the free spirit" makes form into *potentia*, into strength that Emerson defines as eloquence. . . . Fate, as a word, comes from a root meaning "speech," but by one of Emerson's characteristic dialectical reversals Power takes on meaning as eloquent speech while Fate is a script or writing opposed to speech. (*Poems* 7)

Bloom argues that the Emersonian triad of Fate-Freedom-Power appears in Whitman's work as "*my soul-myself-the real me or me myself*" (*Poems* 7). This triad is found in Shepard's work, too, although Freedom, the impulse or spirit which informs writing, is subsumed by Power: Freedom (eloquence) can be expressed only in Power (speech) thereby reducing the Emersonian triad to a pair, Fate and Power. This reduction is important because now the two elements are seen clearly as oppositional: Fate is the antithesis of Power. In this duality, speech is privileged over writing and so is attributed primacy. It is represented as an inchoate, less mediated mode of expression than writing, as having greater capacity to reveal the authentic self. Writing—merely a supplement to the privileged mode of expression, speech—is always secondary.[1]

This tension, although not addressed directly by Shepard, is implied by several remarks he has made. Speaking to the participants in a seminar on playwriting which he taught as part of the Bay Area Playwrights Festival III (1980), Shepard warned, "There is the tendency to trade experience itself for language which never really captures it and ultimately cheats experience" (Wren 81). He suggests that experience is pure but becomes sullied when expressed. Implied by his remark is the position that the plenitude of experience can never be spoken fully. This raises the question: how do we recognize experience except through language?

In "Language, Visualization and the Inner Library," Shepard writes,

> The picture is moving in the mind and being allowed to move more and more freely as you follow it. The following of it is the writing part. In other words, I'm taking notes in as much detail as possible on an event that's happening somewhere inside me. The extent to which I can actually follow the picture and intervene with my own two-cents worth is where inspiration and craftsmanship hold their meaning. If I find myself pushing a character in a certain direction, it's almost a sure sign that I've fallen back on technique and lost the real thread of the thing. (215)

That the writer records the action as it unfolds in his imagination without intervening and shaping it, implies that this action exists independent of and prior to language.

Shepard, while he is reluctant to admit that experience is inseparable from language, is not successful in suppressing the interpretative function of the writer. One of the participants in Shepard's seminar on playwriting, Scott Christopher Wren recalls, "Shepard comments that there is a real sense of following the action from the inside . . ." (85). Again, he insists that experience and language are separate and that language is secondary to experience or, as he says, that it "follows." Subtly, almost imperceptibly, he amends his initial statement of the writer's role:

> . . . There is a real sense of following the action from the inside, such that the accidental gesture has purpose. It's no longer accidental because it's witnessed, followed very carefully moment to moment. (85)

The repetition of "follow" obscures the important shift of ideas in the remark. Initially the writer "follows" the action which implies that action occurs independently and he merely records. What interests me is the ascription of purpose to the gesture because it is the writer who assigns it. The writer no longer follows the scene but witnesses the action and, in so doing, actively enters the scene because in witnessing the action, he reads it. It is the writer who interprets the gesture as significant. Despite his professed belief that action is distinct from language, the ascription of purpose by the writer suggests that Shepard, to some degree, understands them as inseparable. Recognizing action is predicated on our ability to differentiate one action from another which can only be done through categories which are created within language. Shepard's suggestion that the imagination operates independent of language is a bit fanciful; yet, as fanciful as is this idealization of imagination, it is this which informs both Shepard's writing and Whitman's.

Both Whitman and Shepard yearn to discover a language which will make fully present the signified. Necessarily, this language is corporeal, the union of the body (signifier) and spirit (signified) celebrated by the sound of the voice. Wren recalls that Shepard taught "that developing characters is a process of coming in touch with *voice*" (81). He recalls Shepard saying "Voice is the nut of it. Character is an expression of voice, the emotional tone underneath. If a writer is totally connected with the voice, it will be in the words" (76). Shepard's remark implies a sense of character as an essence which is realized only through voice. The breath (spirit) translates this essence from its pure state of interiority to the exteriority of the sign (the actor's body or words).

For Shepard, the crux of the problem of identity is this process of translation. We can only constitute identity through language; but language is debased and so inevitably we lose sight of our "true" or "real" selves. In an interview with Michiko Kakutani, he explained the effect of debased language on identity:

> Personality is everything that is false in a human being. It is everything that's been added on to him and contrived. It seems to me that the struggle all the time is between this sense of falseness and the other haunting sense of what is true—an essential thing that we're born with and tend to lose track of. This naturally sets up a great contradiction in everybody between what they represent and what they know to be themselves. (26)

This nostalgic yearning for an authentic self is perhaps the single most striking feature common both to Shepard's writing and to Whitman's. We need only to think of the title of one of Whitman's poems, "Song of Myself," to recognize the importance of voice to his project of self-representation. The poem is a song which attempts to celebrate masturbation both as an image and inscription of *jouissance* of self-discovery. Here I use "*jouissance*" in Kristeva's sense:

> . . . "Jouissance" is total joy or ecstasy (without any mystical connotation; also, through the working of the signifier, this implies the presence of meaning (jouissance = j'ouis sens = I heard meaning), requiring it by going beyond it. (Roudiez, 16)

"Song of Myself" suggests that the ecstatic moment of orgasm is the moment when the true or essential self is realized fully:

> I merely stir, press, feel with my fingers, and am happy,
> To touch my person to some else's is about as much as I can stand.
> Is then a touch? . . . quivering me to a new identity,
> Flames and ether making a rush for my veins, (616–20)

> ———————————————

> I am given up by traitor:
> I talk wildly. . . . I have lost my wits. . . . I and nobody else am the greatest traitor,
> I went myself first to the headland . . . my own hands carried me there.

> You villain touch! what are you doing? . . . . my breath is tight in its throat;
> unclench your floodgates! you are too much for me. (636–41)

Two aspects of "Song of Myself" are relevant to a discussion of the relationship between Whitman's writing and Shepard's. First, although the poem clearly celebrates masturbation, orgasm is marked by ellipses, by the absence of words. We are given only a description—that the poet talks wildly—but no transcription of what he says. If orgasm is indeed the moment when the true self is realized, then the true self is beyond language. We are reminded of Derrida's contention that the originary moment is beyond knowledge, is always already lost. Secondly, there is the sense of the poet's guilt suggested by the words "traitor" and "villain touch." On the simplest level, it is the expression of self-reproach for daring to acknowledge masturbation. It is the guilt of someone who feels that he is a traitor to himself because he engages in a practice which has been taught, and to some degree believes, is wrong. The expression of guilt divides the self into the traitor and betrayed which, ironically, replicates the onanistic gesture which divides the self into the toucher and the touched thereby recognizing the binary opposition of interiority/exteriority. ". . . The outside, the exposed surface of the body signifies and marks forever the division that shapes auto-affection" (*Grammatology* 165). That the touched surface of the body is exterior insinuates the existence of the interior which remains hidden by the surface. This structure, which recognizes the duality of interior/exterior, is the structure of the sign which is divided into the signified and signifier thus allowing Derrida to claim that "auto affection is a universal structure of experience" (*Grammatology* 165).

For our purposes, what is important about this duality is that knowledge of the interior is possible only through exteriority. The signified is known only through the agency of signifier so that it is never itself present but is always represented. The signified is idealized as that which cannot itself be known. From such a perspective the "real-Me" is beyond knowledge because it cannot be made present. The poet is betrayed by onanism but not simply in the sense of sexual activity. The masturbatory gesture becomes a paradigm for signification because the poet is betrayed by his medium, language, which cannot realize the presence of the "real-Me" that it signifies. Yet, paradoxically, the "real-Me" is idealized only because of the structure of signification which admits the notion of the ideal. The project of making fully present the signified, which is common to Whitman and Shepard, is marked by failure from the outset because the structure of the sign protects the signified as the ideal beyond knowledge. Put simply, once the signified is known, it ceases to be the signified because it is now the signifier.

Chaikin's work never alludes to the influence of American literary figures;[2] however, accounts of his work (particularly in *The Presence of the Actor*) suggest the interest common to his work, Whitman's and Shepard's. The title of Chaikin's book points to his pre-occupation with the notion of "presence;" yet, despite its importance to his work, he never offers an exact definition of the term. Eileen Blumenthal interprets presence as "the quality of being here right now, with an awareness of the actual space and the actual moment of the vital meeting of lives in that space and moment" (113). In contrast,

Chaikin's own description of "presence" is noteworthy for its refusal to define the term with any degree of precision. He writes:

> This "presence" on the stage is a quality given to some and absent from others. All of the history of the theater refers to actors who possess this presence.
>
> It's a quality that makes you feel as though you're sitting in the theatre. . . . There may be nothing of this quality off stage or in any other circumstance in the life of such an actor. It's a deep libidinal surrender which the performer reserves for his anonymous audience. (20)

Later in *The Presence of the Actor* Chaikin writes, "Just before a performance, the actor usually has additional energy like an electrical field" (21). The image of currents of energy recurs:

> . . . The actor must find an empty place where the living current moves through him uninformed. A clear place. Let's say the place from where the breath is drawn . . . not the breath . . . but from where the inhalation starts. . . .
>
> There are streams of human experience which are deep and constant moving through us on a level below sound. As we become occupied with our own noises, we're unable to be in the stream. The more an actor boasts of his feeling as he feels it, the farther he is from the current.
>
> First, the actor must be present in his body, present in his voice . . .
>
> The voice originates inside the body and comes to exist in the room. (66)

These passages illustrate Chaikin's insistence on a lexis of "presence," a lexis which is reminiscent of that developed by Whitman to write the "real Me." "Presence" is a kind of "deep libidinal surrender" which Chaikin renders metaphorically as "the living current." Like Chaikin, Whitman and Shepard use the image of energy to suggest the dynamic, ever-changing and mysterious nature of reality. Whitman, in *Leaves of Grass*, titles a poem "I Sing the Body Electric"; Shepard writes of "Words as tools of imagery in motion" (216) and of a work as having a "life-stream" (Wren 90). For Shepard, the sense of language in motion is particularly important because reality is inconstant. If it is to be made present, it must be done in a flash. "In these lightning-like eruptions words are not thought, they're felt. They cut through space and make perfect sense without having to hesitate for the 'meaning'" (Shepard 217).

In the writings of all three, the image of energy suggests the dynamic, ever-changing nature of reality, constituted as mysterious and unknowable, which relates this reality to identity: in Whitman's poetry, the "real Me" is the originary site of his identity; Shepard claims that through his writing he tries "to go into parts of myself that are unknown" (Lippman 21); Chaikin suggests that the actor attempts to reach an empty place where "the living current moves through him uninformed." Expressed in the work of all three is a nostalgic yearning for a moment of signification when the sign is inseparable from that which it signifies, the condition of language before it has fallen.

The romantic nature of this impulse is suggested by Shepard's remark "that the real quest of a writer is to penetrate into another world" (Shepard 217). Chaikin, too, uses the motif of the quest to describe his work:

> Julian Beck said that an actor has to be like Columbus: he has to go out and discover something, and come back and report on what he discovers. Voyages have to be taken, but there has to be a place to come back to, and this place has to be different from the established theatre. It is not likely to be a business place. (34)

Indeed, in Chaikin's work the quixotic sentiment is so pronounced that it is manifest as a theme. In 1968, the Open Theater performed their collaborative piece, *The Serpent*, which is based on the account of creation in Genesis. "None of us," wrote Chaikin "believe there is or ever was a real Garden of Eden, but it lives in the mind as certain as memory" (67). For Chaikin, the Garden of Eden is not a geographic location now lost but a lost place within each person. Because of the post-lapsarian condition of language, this place cannot be recuperated in language; instead it can only be constituted through the allegoric resonances of myth.

Chaikin's desire to know the Edenic within man replicates Whitman's desire for the "real Me" which Bloom has suggested is a desire for the presexual:

Whitman's "real Me" is what is best and oldest in him, and like the faculty Emerson called "Spontaneity" it is both nature's creation and Whitman's verbal cosmos. It is like a surviving fragment of the original Abyss preceding nature, not Adamic but pre-Adamic. The "real Me" is thus also presexual. ("The Real Me" 6)

The erotic in Whitman's poetry, the longing to express the "real Me" which is presexual, marks the failure of his poetic project. He can never satisfy his desire to retrieve his ideal, presexual self because of the relation between desire and language. Desire is the recognition of absence which is experienced as yearning. Because recognition is possible only through language, desire can only be recognized through language. But, language is itself an expression of desire because the signifier represents, and thus marks the absence of, the signified. That desire should be experienced only through that which is the product of desire is an unresolvable paradox which determines that Whitman can never retrieve his ideal presexual self because language cannot represent that which is presexual.

This problem, which faces Shepard as a writer, is reflected in the characters which he creates. Shepard comments, "Writing is born from a need. A deep burn. If there's no need, there is no desire" (218). He told Michiko Kakutani,

People are starved for the truth and when something comes along that even looks like the truth, people will latch on to it because everything's so false. People are starved for a way of life—they're hunting for a way to be or act toward the world. (26)

Shepard's characters are often so hungry that they speak of themselves as starving. Think, for example, of Shooter in *Action* who says, "I'm starving. Did we eat already?" (139); or, in *Curse of the Starving Class*, of Ella's emphatic declaration to her daughter, "WE'RE HUNGRY, AND THAT'S STARVING ENOUGH FOR ME!" (142); or of the Speaker in *Tongues* who says, "This hunger knows no bounds. This hunger is eating me alive it's so hungry!" (311) and concludes, "Nothing left but the hunger eating itself. Nothing left but the hunger" (312).

The "Hunger Dialogue" is a paradigm for Shepard's use of hunger or appetite throughout his plays. In this piece, hunger is at first the physiological desire for food but, as the dialogue develops, it is clear that the food will not satisfy the speaker's hunger. Indeed, there is nothing which will sate his appetite because he is conscious only of his appetite and cannot identify what it is that he wants. Whether their appetites are for food, for the erotic (as in *Fool for Love* or *A Lie of the Mind,* for example) or the simple desire to tell the true story (for example, in *Buried Child* or *Curse of the Starving Class*), many of Shepard's characters are desirous, their appetites impelling their actions. Yet their desires rarely are satisfied completely, as if the objects of their desire are impossible, which necessarily they are, because the structure of desire is such that desire can never be fully sated. As discussed, desire is recognized only through language which is itself the product of desire. This paradox marks the impossibility of desire being satisfied because the recognition of desire is predicated on language which marks the loss of the full presence of signified.

Invariably the impossible object of the characters' desire is themselves, whom they seek to realize through modes of performance which Florence Falk categorizes as role-playing, story-telling and music-making (188, 189). Shepard comments

> The stories my characters tell are stories that are always unfinished, always imagistic—having to do with recalling experiences through a certain kind of vision. They're always fractured and fragmented and broken. (Kakutani 26)

Given that identity is the story each of us tells about ourselves, the fact that Shepard's characters tell fractured, incomplete stories signals that none of them has a coherent sense of self. In a sense, each tries to call himself into being by performing himself.

As Richard Gilman notes, Shepard's sense of character as ever changing is influenced by Chaikin's work with actors in the Open Theater, particularly the transformation exercises (xv).

> Briefly, a transformation exercise was an improvised scene—a birthday party, survivors in a lifeboat, etc.—in which after a while, and suddenly, the actors were asked to switch immediately to a new scene and therefore wholly new characters.
> . . .

Shepard carried the idea of transformations much farther than the group had by actually writing them into his texts, in plays like *Angel City, Back Bog Beast Bait* and *The Tooth of Crime* where the characters become wholly different in abrupt movements within the course of the work, or speak suddenly as someone else, while the scene may remain the same. (Gilman xv)

The purpose of the transformation exercise is to strip away the actors' contrived sense of how characters behave so that their performances do not rely on theatrical clichés. In theory, this sort of improvisational work encourages the actors to discover different aspects of themselves. As Shepard explains, "The voices of a lot of external-world characters are inside you. For example, when you write about a nun, it's not your 'idea' of a nun, it's the nun inside of you" (Wren 80). Chaikin suggests that each of us has a myriad of characters inside us because within everyone is "a stream of human experiences which are deep and constant" (66). His remark echoes Shepard's answer to Amy Lippman, cited earlier, that the reason he writes is to go into parts of himself which are unknown but are related to everyone (21). In order to reach this place, Chaikin claims that the actor must first "be present in his body, in his own voice" (67); speaking about writing, Shepard corroborates Chaikin's remarks emphasizing "that writers have to begin with what they know and one of the best places is the body because the body is relating to everything and is grounded in experience rather than ideas" (Wren 86). Like Whitman who attempts to inscribe the "real Me" in "Song of Myself," Chaikin and Shepard use the analogy of music, in their case jazz, to explain how an actor will realize character. Chaikin suggests jamming a structure for improvisational work:

The term comes from jazz, from the jam session. One actor comes in and moves in contemplation of a theme, traveling within rhythms, going through and out of the phrasing, sometimes using just the gesture, sometimes reducing the whole thing to pure sound. . . . During the jamming, if the performers let it, the theme moves into associations, a combination of free and structured form. (116)

In *Angel City*, jamming became Shepard's structural principle for the creation character. He instructs,

> The term "character" could be thought of in a different way when working on this play. Instead of the idea of a "whole character" with logical motives behind this behaviour which the actor submerges himself into, he should consider instead a fractured whole with bits and pieces of character flying off the central theme. In other words, more in terms of collage construction or jazz improvisation. (6)

As Florence Falk explains, "jazz in its very structure is improvisational—that is an alert, spontaneous, and dynamic creation" (190). It operates, as Shepard noted about rock music in the program note to *Cowboy Mouth*, on a physical level which allows (or at any rate gives the illusion of allowing) the union of impulse and expression: the signified is one with the signifier. Writing techniques based on jazz inhibit the mediation imposed by intellectualizing the process of writing. "When you're writing inside of a character like this, you aren't pausing every ten seconds to figure out what it all means," explains Shepard (217). We are returned to Shepard's sense of the writer following and recording the action.

Shepard's quest for an ideal language which will make fully present the signified clearly situates his project within the larger frame of American culture. "Presence" is not simply an attitude towards language but indicates no ideology which informs many aspects of this culture. It is manifest thematically as popular images of the frontier which is the borderline between civilization and wilderness. The frontier is a myth of eternal presence because when the frontier is encroached upon either by wilderness or civilization, it is not transformed but moves and is reconstituted in a new location. A frontier is always the same, is always the borderline. There may be a history of frontiers, but the frontier is itself a place without history because it is unchanging. In this sense the myth of the frontier enacts spatially the transcendentalist poetics to which Shepard is heir because the writer's desire is the discovery of a language which is pure, at the borderline when utterance is first made, "no longer a shout but not yet discourse."

Shepard's celebrated language is realized through his recurring interest in the West of popular culture (as, for example, in *Angel City*, *The Tooth of Crime*, *The Unseen Hand*). This thematic preoccupation exposes the ideological implications of presence in his work. First, the frontier is the domain of the cowboy who, as he is popularly represented, affirms the pre-adolescent values of a white, American boy. The sensibility is "usually anti-intellectual and anti-school" and so physical prowess is counted upon to resolve any conflict or problem (Davis 94–95). His strongest emotional tie (other than to his horse) is to

> a group of buddies, playing poker, chasing horse thieves, riding in masculine company. He is contemptuous of farmers, has no interest in children, and considers men who have lived among women as effete. Usually he left his own family at a tender age and rebelled against the restrictions of mothers and older sisters. (Davis 89)

Bonnie Marranca notes that the determination of the frontier myth is evident in Shepard's characterization of women:

> One of the most problematic aspects of the plays is Shepard's consistent refusal or inability, whichever the case may be, to create female characters whose imaginative range matches that of the males. . . . For a young man Shepard's portrayal of women is as outdated as the frontier ethic he celebrates: men have their showdowns or face the proverbial abyss while the women are absorbed in simple activities and simplistic thoughts. (30)

The pre-pubescent impulse of the myth casts women as dominating figures (mothers and sisters who are rebelled against) who want to rob men of their masculinity. In reaction to this fear of woman, the myth contains her by casting her as the complement to men. A woman, in westerns, is simply the site for a man to express tenderness. She "brings out qualities in him which we could not see otherwise. Without her, he would be too much the brute for a real folk hero, at least in the modern age" (Davis 89; Marranca 31).

In a broader political context, the myth of the frontier has important implications for Shepard's work. Although cowboys belong to gangs, these fraternal groups are devoid of any political (as distinct from moral) consciousness. The fact that the frontier is a borderline informs all aspects of life there. The social structures are informal, neither wilderness which has no social order nor civilization which is highly ordered but the liminality of emerging social organization. The structure of this paradigm replicates that of the transcendentalist's language which is seen as the threshold, "no longer a shout but not yet discourse." What is paradoxical is that the ideology of "present"—as it is articulated in the myth of the frontier and in the poetics of the transcendentalism—inscribes a politic which is both radical and conservative. It is radical because the individual is allowed to realize himself fully, unencumbered by social restraint; yet, the project is predicated on the existence of ideals which are accepted uncritically: the "true" self which can be realized; the triumph of good as the moral imperative of the frontier where the cowboy in the white hat always wins.

Shepard's romantic belief in the "true" self which is betrayed by language tends toward, if not conservatism, at least an apolitical perspective. The individual turns inward to discover himself rather than outward to the world in which he lives. Shepard's characters almost never indicate any sense of themselves as socially constructed beings. Perhaps by simple virtue of some concern for issues related to "class" as indicated by the title, *Curse of the Starving Class* comes closest to exploring the social determination of character. Yet even in that play, political concerns are transformed into concerns about performance. Faced with losing their land, the characters deny their situation by retreating into the world of fiction and memory as they tell the story of the eagle and the cat, even as the world around them literally and metaphorically blows up.

The concern with performance over politics characterizes all Shepard's work and is particularly important given his thematic pre-occupation with the West. Shepard is critical of aspects of the West, for example, the new West represented by the film industry of Hollywood which manufactures images that delude people, thereby denying their realization of their identities. He does not examine, however, the relation of the new West to the old. The Old West, in which Shepard so delights, was generated by Hollywood and bears little relation to the historical reality.[3] This mythical West where men are men and women are their complements (and everybody is white) is surely not the place where the "true" self can be realized. Or perhaps this is the final paradox: the "true" self can be realized through fiction.

References

Bloom, Harold. *Poems of Our Climate*. Ithaca: Cornell University Press, 1976.

―――. "The Real Me." Review of *Walt Whitman: The Making of the Poet* by Paul Zweig, *The New York Review of Books* 31, no. 7 (April 26, 1984).

Blumenthal, Eileen. "Joseph Chaikin: An Open Theory of Acting," *Yale/Theater* 8, nos. 2 and 3 (Spring 1977): 112–33.

Chaikin, Joseph. *The Presence of the Actor*. New York: Atheneum, 1972.

Davis, David Brion. "Ten Gallon Hero." *Myth and the American Experience*. Vol. 2. Ed. Nicholas Gage and Patrick Gerster. New York: Glencoe Press, 1973.

Derrida, Jacques. *Of Grammatology*. Trans. Gayatri Chakravorty Spivak. Baltimore: Johns Hopkins University, 1976.

―――. "The Supplement to Copula: Philosophy *before* Linguistics." *Textual Strategies*. Ed. Josue Harari. Ithaca: Cornell University Press, 1979.

―――. "The Theater of Cruelty." *Writing and Difference*. Trans. Alan Bass. Chicago: University of Chicago Press, 1980.

Durham, Philip. "The Cowboy and the Myth Makers," *Journal of Popular Culture* 1, no. 1 (Summer 1967): 58–62.

Earley, Michael. "Of Life Immense in Passion, Pulse and Power." *American Dreams: The Imagination of Sam Shepard*. Ed. Bonnie Marranca. New York: Performing Arts Journal Publications, 1981, pp. 126–33.

Falk, Florence. "The Role of Performance in Sam Shepard's Plays," *Theatre Journal* 33, no. 2 (May 1981): 182–98.

Gilman, Richard. Introduction. *Seven Plays* by Sam Shepard. New York: Bantam Books, 1981.

Kakutani, Michiko. "Myths, Dreams, Realities—Sam Shepard's America," *The New York Times*, 29 January 1984, Section 2.

Lippman, Amy. "A Conversation with Sam Shepard," *The Harvard Advocate* (March 1983). Reprinted *Gamut* 5 (January 1984): 10–28.

Marranca, Bonnie. "Alphabetical Shepard: The Play of Words." *American Dreams: The Imagination of Sam Shepard*. Ed. Bonnie Marranca. New York: Performing Arts Journal Publications, 1981, pp. 13–34.

Roudiez, Leon S. Introduction. *Desire in Language: A Semiotic Approach to Literature and Art.* Ed. Leon S. Roudiez. Trans. Thomas Gora, Alice Jardine and Leon S. Roudiez. New York: Columbia University Press, 1980.

Shewey, Don. *Sam Shepard.* New York: Dell, 1985.

———. *Curse of the Starving Class. Seven Plays* by Sam Shepard. New York: Bantam Books, 1981.

———. "Language, Visualization and the Inner Library." *The Drama Review* 21, no. 4 (December 1977): 49–58. Reprinted in *American Dreams: The Imagination of Sam Shepard.* Ed. Bonnie Marranca. New York: Performing Arts Journal Publications, 1981.

———, and Joseph Chaikin. *Tongues. Seven Plays.* By Sam Shepard. New York: Performing Arts Journal Publications, 1981.

Whitman, Walt. *Leaves of Grass.* Harmondsworth: Penguin Books, 1981. Fp. in Brooklyn, 1855.

Wren, Scott Christopher. "Camp Shepard: Exploring the Geography of Character." *West Coast Plays* 7 (1980): 71–106.

Notes

1. For a fuller discussion of the notion of the supplement see: Jacques Derrida, "The Supplement of Copula: Philosophy *before* Linguistics," *Textual Strategies,* ed. Josue Harari (Ithaca: Cornell University Press, 1979), 82–121.
2. In *Presence of the Actor,* Chaikin cites theatre practitioners as having the greatest influence on his work. These include: Nola Chilton, Mira Roshiva, Judith Malina and Julian Beck, members of the Open Theater (45).
3. Historically, the age of the cowboy is brief: from the period just after the American Civil War until just after 1874 when barbed wire was invented. With the invention of barbed wire, ranches were fenced in and the work of the cowboy became redundant. "The early cowboys were Texans—white, Negro, and Mexican, but outsiders of almost every nationality were also represented." Philip Durham,

"The Cowboy and the Myth Makers," *Journal of Popular Culture* 1, No. 1 (Summer 1967): 58.

WORKING FOR SAM

Tommy Thompson

One evening, five or six years ago, my fellow Red Clay Ramblers and I were cramped up in a small orange van full of guitars and what all, travelling southeast from Calgary. We'd driven straight through the first night, through the next day, slept six hours that night, and after fourteen hours today, were hankering for a cheap motel. A good sleep now would allow just time for us to play the last scheduled concert two days hence at Northern Iowa University. We were having an argument because I'd promised the public radio station on the campus we would arrive a day early and do a live broadcast (for no pay). I support public radio. Besides, I thought the radio exposure would help promote our concert. "We don't go without sleep to give free shows," some said. "Exposure is what people die of." We were tired, and it was a foolish promise. But all agreed it was too late now to break it. So we pressed on for twenty-two more hours, glum and smelly as hostages, arrived at the station minutes before air time, and gave them a show.

I don't think the radio helped our concert, though. It was held next day at the student union. In the dining hall at noon. We've had some bizarre gigs in our time, but never before in a student dining hall while lunch was dispensed by fast food franchises. It was a fine turnout, but we weren't the main attraction.

As it turned out, the radio show had been worth the trouble. The station folks dealt with our tardy and disgruntled arrival with friendly efficiency. They'd pulled in a small enthusiastic audience of RCR fans, the sound reinforcement was fine, and, somewhere out there in the middle of Iowa, Sam Shepard was listening.

That was in 1982, and Sam was on location for the filming of the movie *Country*. In the fall of 1985, he was in New York directing the premier production of his new play, *A Lie of the Mind*. It's his practice to mix music with theatre, and this time he intended to use the recorded singing of two "high lonesome" primitives, Skip James and Roscoe Holcomb. For some reason he changed his mind, decided that only live music would properly serve the show. He remembered us—somebody said he noticed the band's name on an old *Diamond Studs* poster— phone calls were made, deals discussed, and two of us flew to New York to meet the man with the right stuff.

Rehearsals were under way on the second floor of a former church in midtown Manhattan. We sat for twenty minutes in a hallway while a ticklish scene was refined in privacy. Then the door opened, Sam stood to greet us, we introduced ourselves, he introduced us to the cast, and we all took a coffee break together. Whatever I might have imagined such an event to be like, it was blessedly comfortable and ordinary. Just a roomful of extraordinary actors drinking bad coffee out of styrofoam cups.

We watched the rest of the rehearsals that day and had our first private meeting with Sam. He'd listened to our records, chosen a few songs, and had ideas for others he wanted us to write. It became clear that we weren't being interviewed for the job; it was already ours. That is to say, two weeks into rehearsals, months after the budget had been set, Sam had induced the producers to hire a five-member band they'd never heard of, *and* hire a sound technician, *and* reduce the paid seating to make space for us, *and* redesign the lighting to make us visible.

We moved ourselves to New York and spent October and November writing, selecting, arranging, and rehearsing songs and instrumental music to support the stage action. Sam had his hands full as a director with eight experienced, more or less tractable actors, and a too-long script (the first run-through ran six hours). Sometimes he seemed more at home with us than with the cast. He is a musician himself and knows the language. And, of course, we were bending over backwards with tractability.

Sam has a good sense of how a roughed-in piece of music will eventually work when it's been refined and placed. He looks for the emotional content of a scene or moment and avoids "character themes" and dramatic clichés. He asked us to write or find songs that made no direct reference to the play's action or characters. He wanted music that felt old, music that would carry his notion that the same absurd and dreadful conflicts have plagued families forever. Often as not, he would ask for a song or melody that, instead of supporting an actor's lines, would undercut it with irony.

Distance is what Sam understands. Music too much like the action is redundant. Too dissimilar and it's misleading, He always found the exact distance. We made some pretty good music for *A Lie of the Mind*, much better than it would have been without Sam's intuitive artistry.

The show opened in early December of 1985. After the second performance, Sam met us backstage to say good-bye. The usual compliments and thanks were exchanged, and then, as he was about to go, he said we'd work together again, "We'll do a film." That's a sentence a person can say softly with his mouth barely open. After a couple of years, we began to wonder if he *had* said it.

But we did do a movie. It's called *Far North*, written and directed by Sam Shepard, starring Jessica Lange, and scheduled for release in the fall of 1988. Once again, Sam had gone to his producers and said, "These are the guys who are doing the score." Period.

After years of struggle, Sam has earned his fair share of power. We've twice been its grateful beneficiaries. But it's not power that's so admirable. It's courage. He knew something of our music, that first time around, but he had no certainty we'd be able to give his play what it needed. And when the movie came along, the stakes were higher, the technology more exotic, and the producers more skeptical. What if we screwed up? Sam would have been the first to say, "This is no good; this won't work." What a mess! And all on his head.

In the end, Sam's commitment was not to producers and investors, and not to us, but to his own vision. He's earned the power to realize that vision and has courage enough to use it. Fortunately for us all, it's the vision of a great artist.

I'm glad to say that "Great Artist" is not a day-to-day role Sam is inclined to play. Once, in the early stages of the film score, he spent some time with us in Chapel Hill. He wanted guitar on one of the cues, and he thought "chicken pickin' " would be the perfect rhythm. He borrowed Jack's guitar, and while we watched the scene on video, Sam gave us a sample of chicken pickin'. Somehow, it wasn't working.

Instruments began to be traded around, and . . . well, let me leave you with a picture of great art in the making. Chris and Bland and I formed the audience, Jack played guitar, Clay played mandolin, and Sam sat in a straight-back chair slapping rhythm on his thighs and tapping the beat on a sauce pan with the toe of his cowboy boot. It sounded fine.

BIBLIOGRAPHY

Primary Works

I. PLAYS

Action. Staged London, 1974; New York, 1975. In *Action and The Unseen Hand*. London: Faber and Faber, 1975.

Angel City. Staged San Francisco, 1976. In *Angel City and Other Plays*. New York, Urizen Press, 1976.

Blue Bitch. Staged New York, 1973.

Buried Child. Staged New Haven and New York, 1978. Pulitzer Prize. In *Buried Child and Seduced and Suicide in B Flat*. New York: Urizen Books, 1979.
———. In *Seven Plays*. Toronto: Bantam, 1981.

Chicago. Staged New York, 1965. In *Eight Plays from Off-Off Broadway*. Ed. Nick Orzel and Michael T. Smith. Indianapolis: Bobbs-Merrill, 1966.
———. In *Five Plays*. Indianapolis: Bobbs-Merrill, 1967, 1981.
———. In *Five Plays*. London: Faber and Faber, 1969.

Cowboy Mouth (with Patti Smith). Staged New York, 1971. In *Mad Dog Blues and Other Plays*. New York: Winter House, 1971.
———. In *Winter Repertory* 4 (1972).

Cowboys. Staged New York, 1964.

Cowboys #2. Staged Los Angeles, 1967. In *Collision Course*. Ed. Edward Parone. New York: Random House, 1968.

————. In *Mad Dog Blues and Other Plays*. New York: Winter House, 1971.

————. In *Winter Repertory* 4 (1972).

Curse of the Starving Class. Staged London, 1977; New York, 1978. In *Angel City and Other Plays*. New York: Urizen Press, 1976.

————. In *Seven Plays*. Toronto: Bantam, 1981.

Dog. Staged New York, 1965.

Fool for Love. Staged San Francisco, 1983; New York, 1983. In *Fool for Love and The Sad Lament of Pecos Bill on the Eve of Killing his Wife*. San Francisco: City Light Books, 1983.

Forensic and the Navigators. Staged New York, 1967. In *The Best of Off-Off Broadway*. Ed. Michael T. Smith. New York: Dutton, 1969.

————. In *The Unseen Hand and Other Plays*. Indianapolis: Bobbs-Merrill, 1971.

4-H Club. Staged New York, 1965. In *Mad Dog Blues and Other Plays*. New York: Winter House, 1971.

Fourteen Hundred Thousand. Staged Minneapolis, 1966. In *Five Plays*. Indianapolis: Bobbs-Merrill, 1967, 1981.

————. In *Five Plays*. London: Faber and Faber, 1969.

Geography of a Horse Dreamer. Staged New Haven, 1974. In *The Tooth of Crime, and Geography of a Horse Dreamer*. New York: Grove Press, 1974; London: Faber and Faber, 1974.

————. In *Four Two Act Plays*. London: Faber, 1974.

Holy Ghostly. Staged New York, 1970. In *The Unseen Hand and Other Plays*. Indianapolis: Bobbs-Merrill, 1971.

————. In *Best Short Plays of the World Theatre 1968-1973*. Ed. Stanley Richards. New York: Crown, 1973.

Icarus's Mother. Staged New York, 1965. In *Five Plays*. Indianapolis: Bobbs-Merrill, 1967, 1981.

————. In *Five Plays*. London: Faber and Faber, 1969.

Inacoma. Staged San Francisco, 1977.

Jacaranda (a libretto). Produced New York, 1979.

Killer's Head. Staged New York, 1975.

La Turista. Staged New York, 1967. Indianapolis: Bobbs-Merrill, 1968.

————. London: Faber and Faber, 1969.

————. In *Four Two Act Plays.* Indianapolis: Bobbs-Merrill, 1980.

————. In *Seven Plays.* Toronto: Bantam, 1981.

A Lie of the Mind. Staged New York, 1985. In *A Lie of the Mind and The War in Heaven: Angel's Monologue.* New York: New American Library, 1987.

Little Ocean. Staged London, 1974.

Mad Dog Blues. Staged New York, 1971. In *Mad Dog Blues and Other Plays.* New York: Winter House, 1971.

Melodrama Play. Staged New York, 1966. In *Five Plays.* Indianapolis: Bobbs-Merrill, 1967, 1981.

————. In *Five Plays.* London: Faber and Faber, 1969.

Nightwalk (with Megan Terry and Jean-Claude van Itallie). Staged New York, 1973.

Operation Sidewinder. Staged New York, 1970. In *Esquire*, May 1969.

————. Indianapolis: Bobbs-Merrill, 1970.

————. In *The Great American Life Show.* Ed. John Lahr and J. Price. New York: Bantam, 1976.

————. In *Four Two Act Plays.* Indianapolis: Bobbs-Merrill, 1980.

Red Cross. Staged New York, 1966. In *Five Plays.* Indianapolis: Bobbs-Merrill, 1967, 1981.

————. In *Five Plays.* London: Faber and Faber, 1969.

Rock Garden. Staged New York, 1964; excerpt in *Oh! Calcutta*, New York, 1969.

————. In *The Unseen Hand and Other Plays.* Indianapolis: Bobbs-Merrill, 1971.

————. In *Scripts*, 1 (January 1972): 24–30.

————. In *Winter Repertory* 4 (1972).

Rocking Chair. Staged New York, 1965.

Savage/Love (with Joseph Chaikin). Staged San Francisco, 1978; New York, 1979.
————. In *Seven Plays*. Toronto: Bantam, 1981.

Seduced. Staged Providence, 1978; New York, 1979. In *Buried Child and Seduced and Suicide in B Flat*. New York: Urizen Press, 1979.

Shaved Splits. Staged New York, 1969. In *The Unseen Hand and Other Plays*. Indianapolis: Bobbs-Merrill, 1971.

Suicide in B Flat. Staged New York, 1976. In *Buried Child and Seduced and Suicide in B Flat*. New York: Urizen Press, 1979.

Terminal. Written with Megan Terry and Jean-Claude van Itallie in 1971.

Tongues (with Joseph Chaikin). Staged San Francisco, 1978; New York, 1979.
————. In *Seven Plays*. Toronto: Bantam, 1981.

The Tooth of the Crime. Staged London, 1972; Oswego N.Y., and New York, 1973. In *Performance* 5 (March-April 1973): 67–91.
————. In *The Tooth of Crime, and Geography of a Horse Dreamer*. New York: Grove Press, 1974.
————. In *Four Two Act Plays*. Indianapolis: Bobbs-Merrill, 1980.
————. In *Four Two Act Plays*. London: Faber and Faber, 1974.
————. In *Seven Plays*. Toronto: Bantam, 1981.

True Dylan. A one-act play published in *Esquire*, July 1987.

True West. Staged New York, 1980. In *Seven Plays*. Toronto: Bantam, 1981.

The Unseen Hand. Staged New York, 1970. Toronto: Bantam, 1986.
————. In *The Unseen Hand and Other Plays*. Indianapolis: Bobbs-Merrill, 1971.
————. In *Plays and Players* 20 (May 1973): i–xi.
————. In *Action and the Unseen Hand*. London: Faber and Faber, 1975.

Up to Thursday. Staged New York, 1965.

The War in Heaven: Angel's Monologue. A radio play, with Joseph Chaikin. Produced in 1985.

II. OTHER WORKS

Hawkmoon: A Book of Short Stories, Poems, and Monologues. New York: Performing Arts Journal Publications, 1981.
————. Los Angeles: Black Sparrow Press, 1973.

Me and My Brother. A screenplay written with Robert Frank, 1971.

"Metaphors, Mad Dogs and Old-Time Cowboys." *Theatre Quarterly* 4 (August-October, 1974): 3–16. Shepard traces his career as a playwright and director.

Motel Chronicles. San Francisco: City Light Books, 1982. Poetry and prose.

"OOB and the Playwright: Two Commentaries." Written with Tom Sankly. *Works* 1 (Winter 1968): 70–73. Shepard discusses why he prefers OOB (Off-Off Broadway) to more established theater.

Paris, Texas. A screenplay written with Wim Wenders. Berlin: Road Movies, 1984.

Ringaleevio. A screenplay written with Murray Mednick in 1971.

Rolling Thunder Logbook. A record of a tour made with Bob Dylan and Allen Ginsberg in 1976. New York: Viking, 1977.

Sad Lament of Pecos Bill on the Eve of Killing His Wife. In *Fool for Love and The Sad Lament of Pecos Bill on the Eve of Killing His Wife.* San Francisco: City Light Books, 1983.

"Sam Shepard, Playwright." *Performing Arts Journal* 26 (Fall 1977): 13–24. Shepard writes about theater and its relationship to recent changes in American culture. He also discusses the need for experimental theatre.

"Time." *Theatre* (New Haven) 9 (Spring 1978): 9. Shepard writes about commercial pressures on playwrights.

"Visualization, Language and the Inner Library." *Drama Review* 21 (December 1977): 49–58. Shepard talks about his composing process.

Major Criticism

Aaron, J. "Angel City," *Educational Theatre Journal* 29 (October 1977): 415–16.
This article discusses the effect of the American movie culture on theatre, focusing on three plays. *Merton of the Movies* by George S. Kaufman and Marc Connelly, and *A History of the American Film* by Christopher Durang, are compared to Shepard's *Angel City*. In all three the socialization and corruption of America by Hollywood are subjects for disturbing satire.

Albee, Edward. *"Icarus's Mother," Village Voice,* 25 November 1965, 19.
Albee believes in Shepard's talent but has mixed feelings about his craftsmanship.

Auerbach, Doris. *Sam Shepard, Arthur Kopit, and the Off-Broadway Theatre.* Boston: Twayne, 1982.
Auerbach follows Shepard's career up through 1979, and provides a good introduction to his life and work. She also gives a history of Off-Broadway theatre.

Bachman, Charles R. "Defusion of Menace in the Plays of Sam Shepard," *Modern Drama* 19 (December 1976): 405–16.
Bachman has written one of the most sustained and perceptive analyses of Shepard's work, praising his transformation of "the original stereotyped characters and situations into an imaginative, linguistically brilliant, quasi-surrealistic chemistry of text and stage presentation which is original and authentically his own." Bachman considers *Chicago, Cowboy Mouth, Tooth of the Crime,* and *Forensic and the Navigators* Shepard's best plays because the theme of menace in each is undiluted by the force of surrealism that mars many of his works.

Blumenthal, Eileen. "Chaikin and Shepard Speak in Tongues." *Village Voice,* 26 November 1979, 103.

This interview with both playwrights delineates their cooperation. Shepard says that he "feels like an apprentice" to Chaikin. The article indicates that *Tongues* and *Savage/Love* were each written and prepared for production in three weeks.

Chubb, K. "Fruitful Difficulties of Directing Shepard." *Theatre Quarterly* 4 (August 1974): 17–25.

Chubb, director of the Wakefield Tricycle Theatre Company, claims success in directing Shepard's plays, noting that he respected the playwright's theatricality and sincerity. Shepard's sense of what is theatrically effective "goes beyond rules and preconceptions." The lack of traditional structure in his plays has frustrated many directors, including Charles Marowitz and Richard Schechner. Chubb suggests one must intuit Shepard's intentions.

Cima, Jay Gibson. "Shifting Perspectives: Combining Shepard and Rauschenberg." *Theatre Journal* 38.1 (1986): 67–81.

Cima notes the similarities between Shepard's plays and artist Robert Rauschenberg's "combines," his combinations of sculpture and painting. Both artists' works feature odd juxtapositions and ambiguity, and it is difficult to determine a frame. Cima encourages audiences to approach Shepard's plays with the same sense of playfulness they would bring to a viewing of Rauschenberg's art.

Coe, Robert. "Saga of Sam Shepard," *New York Times Magazine*, 23 November 1980, pp. 56–58, 118, 120, 122, 124.

The article focuses on character and biography, with Coe seeing the playwright-actor turned cow-puncher and rodeo rider as a recluse from the theatrical mainstream. He comments on Shepard's fascination with myth, his original voice, his vernacular rhythms, and his preoccupation with family plays. *True West*, a play about two brothers, extends one of Shepard's persistent themes, "the dislocation and impermanence which has characterized the American experience since World War II." The latter part of the article includes biographical data: Shepard's work in England, off-Off-Broadway, and now with San Francisco's Magic Theatre. In all his work Shepard reflects "his experience of a wilderness where America has always hidden its promise and its dream."

Cohn, Ruby. "Sam Shepard," in *Contemporary Dramatists*. Ed. James Vinson. London: St. James Press; New York: St. Martin's Press, 1973, 722–23.

Cohn focuses mainly on Shepard's language, particularly his command of slang. Shepard has absorbed American pop art, media myths, and the Southwestern Scene, "and created image-focused plays in which the characters speak inventive idioms in vivid rhythms." She singles out *The Tooth of the Crime, La Turista,* and *Mad Dog Blues* for special praise.

Davis, R.A. " 'Get up Out a' Your Homemade Beds': The Plays of Sam Shepard," *Players* 47 (1972): 12–19.
In a critical piece, Davis laments the thematic poverty of Shepard's plays, all of which deal monotonously with the need for the individual to find a temporary shelter in a harsh world. Nevertheless, Davis comments on Shepard's brilliant theatricality.

Fennell, Patrick J. "Angel City," *Educational Theatre Journal* 29 (March 1977): 112–13.
Fennell offers a review of *Angel City,* but also goes beyond that to discuss Shepard's ability to work with mixed media—in this case with film and music—as well as stage action. He notes the recurrent theme of the artist destroyed by success, also apparent in *The Tooth of the Crime* and *Suicide in B Flat.*
————. "Sam Shepard: The Flesh and Blood of Theatre," *Dissertation Abstracts* 38 (1977): 3145A.
Fennell's dissertation covers twenty-seven plays in a wide-ranging study. He devotes a chapter each to Shepard's theatricalism, his use of the "transformations situation," his use of magic (including ritual and trance), his varied language (various forms of slang, Pinteresque ellipses, and futuristic jargon) and his reliance on the media.

Frutkin, Ren. "Sam Shepard: Paired Existence Meets the Monster, *Yale/Theatre* 2 (Spring 1969): 22–30.
Discussing *Cowboys #2* and *La Turista,* Frutkin argues that the central subject of theater in 1969 is the "value of performance." By "performance" he means "the shared style of a generation, the theatricalization of everyday life." Frutkin believes that Shepard is trying to save his audiences from confusing role-playing with life, by "theatrically rescuing the imagination from total theatricalization."

Gelber, Jack. "Sam Shepard: The Playwright as Shaman," Introduction to *Angel City and Other Plays,* by Sam Shepard. New York: Urizen Books, 1976, 1–4.
Gelber holds that Shepard's plays are dramatic "trips," that his characters are "on trips," and that the plays themselves "are in the form of trips, quests, adventures." Saying that Shepard is as American as peyote, magic mushrooms, and rock and roll, Gelber insists that Shepard

is the modern equivalent of a primitive shaman who "directly confronts the supernatural for purposes of cures."

Goldbery, Robert. "Sam Shepard, Off-Broadway's Street Cowboy," *College Papers* (Winter 1980): 43–45.
This interview covers all of the usual questions about background, work, and friends. Shepard's answers include some interesting sidelights on drugs and the '60s, the role of music, especially jazz, in his work, and Patti Smith's influence on his writing. Shepard calls Leroi Jones (Amiri Baraka) the greatest American playwright and Peter Handke "the best in the world" after Beckett. Of his craft, Shepard says: "I write because it's thrilling."

Hart, Linda. *Sam Shepard's Metaphysical Stages*. New York: Greenwood, 1987.
After a useful biographical sketch, the book discusses ten of Shepard's plays, from *Cowboys #2* to *A Lie of the Mind*, emphasizing the playwright's development. Hart attempts to "connect his drama to recognizable tradition." There is also a discussion of the connection between Shepard's plays and his work in movies.

Kleb, William. "Shepard and Chaikin Speaking in *Tongues*," *Theatre* (New Haven) 10 (February 1978): 66–69.
Kleb praises the performance of *Tongues* at San Francisco's Magic Theatre by Shepard and Joseph Chaikin.

Kramer, Mimi. "In Search of the Good Shepard," *The New Criterion* 2 , No. 2 (Oct. 1983): 51–57.
Kramer discusses the playwright's relationship to his audience, and the common image of Shepard as "shaman." She says he "teeters dangerously on the brink of ritualism," and complains that most discussions of Shepard have left "the realm of rational discourse."

Kroll, Jack. "Crazy Henry," *Newsweek*, 8 May 1978, 94.
In his review of *Seduced*, Kroll notes the play's "view of the madness of the drive for power," and calls Shepard "the most American" of our playwrights.

Lion, John. "Rock 'n Roll Jesus with a Cowboy Mouth: Sam Shepard is the Inkblot of the '80s," *American Theatre* 1, No. 1 (April 1984): 4–8.
Lion believes there are similarities among Alan Ginsberg, Elvis Presley, and Sam Shepard. Each reflects his period of American life.

Lippman, Amy. "Rhythms and Truths," *American Theatre* 1, No. 1, (April 1984): 9–13, 40–41.

Originally published in March 1983 in *The Harvard Advocate*, this interview with Shepard covers a wide range of topics, but keeps circling back to the issue of his composing process.

Marranca, Bonnie. "Alphabetical Shepard," *Performing Arts Journal* 5 (1981): 9–25.

Offering a sort of lexicon to Shepard's works, Marranca defines certain terms which characterize Shepard's approach to theater, such as "geographies of the spirit" and "the rhythm of imagery." She says Shepard holds the "radical ideal of an authorless work and the denial of the Author as Myth." He substitutes myth for history and experience for theory.

————, ed. *American Dreams: The Imagination of Sam Shepard.* New York: Performing Arts Journal Publications, 1981.

This is a kaleidoscopic collection of material. In an introduction, Marranca discusses Shepard's "play of words," noting his use of music. There are fourteen critical essays, written as early as 1965 and as late as 1981. There are also five essays written from a production point of view: three about directing and two about acting. Finally, there are selections from Shepard interviews.

Mazzocco, Robert. "Sam Shepard's Big Roundup," *The New York Review of Books* 32, No. 8 (9 May 1985): 21–27.

This is a survey of Shepard's work as a reflection of American culture. Mazzocco pays especial attention to Shepard's use of Eden mythology.

Mottram, Ron. *Inner Landscapes: The Theatre of Sam Shepard.* Columbia: University of Missouri, 1984.

Mottram provides a critical overview of Shepard's career, proceeding chronologically. Mottram makes special use of Shepard's prose and poetry as ways into understanding the plays. This is a useful biographical and critical study.

Nash, Thomas. "Sam Shepard's *Buried Child*: The Ironic Use of Folklore," *Modern Drama* 26.4 (1983): 486–91.

Nash analyzes the ritual qualities of *Buried Child* while illustrating how the play conforms to the mythological pattern of the death and rebirth of the Corn King.

Powe, Bruce W. *"The Tooth of Crime*: Sam Shepard's Way with Music," *Modern Drama* 24, No. 1 (March 1981): 39–46.
Powe quotes Patti Smith's phrase "the poetry of Speed" to describe the musical tenor of Shepard's plays. Powe analyzes Shepard's connection to a specific element of our *zeitgeist*—rock music.

Rosen, Carol. "Sam Shepard's *Angel City*: A Movie for the Stage," *Modern Drama* 22 (March 1979): 39–46.
Rosen's real interest here is Shepard's translation of film techniques—jump-cuts, splicing, etc.—to the stage, all quite appropriate in *Angel City* which is set in a movie studio. Rosen calls Shepard a "playwright of zap-pop-pow action" and of "comic book verbs." Shepard's plays often depict movies as the ultimate drug, dulling the ethical and moral values of the public.

"Sam Shepard: Writer on the Way Up," *New York Times*, 12 November 1969, p. 42:1.
This article gives a sense of Shepard's popularity in New York at that time.

Schechner, Richard. "Drama, Script, Theatre, Performance," *Drama Review* 17 (September 1973): 5–36.
Schechner uses Shepard's *The Tooth of Crime* as an example of the breakdown of barriers between illusion and reality in the theatre. Until recently drama in the Western world preceded the script. The reversal of this process limits the effectiveness of theatre: "The drama is the domain of the author. . . the script. . . of the teacher."

Simon, John. "Soft Centers," *New York* 16 (13 June 1983): 76–77.
Simon gives a negative review of *Fool for Love*: "What dominates here . . . is the absence, the powerful absence of discipline, Shepard's besetting sin."
———. "Theatre Chronicle: Kopit, Norman, and Shepard," *Hudson Review* 32 (Spring 1979): 77–88.
Simon brilliantly connects these three very different plays by showing that in each "language is the least important element" and that the characters in all these plays have split personalities. He finds the meaning of *Buried Child* elusive but records the disturbing power of the playwright's symbols and images.

Smith, Michael. "Theatre: *Cowboys* and *The Rock Garden*," *The Village Voice*, 22 October 1964, 13.

This favorable review of Shepard's first two productions is extremely significant, because it gave Shepard the confidence to continue writing, despite generally disparaging criticism. Smith says that Theatre Genesis has "actually found a new playwright," one "with an intuitive approach to language and dramatic structure and moving into an area between ritual and naturalism."

Smith, Patti. "Sam Shepard: 9 Random Years (7 + 2)," Poem in *Angel City and Other Plays*. New York: Urizen Press, 1976, 241-45.
Smith has written a "biographical" poem which recounts Shepard's love-life experiences. It captures the spirit of many of Shepard's plays.

Stambolian, George. "Shepard's *Mad Dog Blues*: A Trip Through Popular Culture," *Journal of Popular Culture* 7: 777–86.
Stambolian believes that in all of his plays Shepard is searching for "a new mythology," which will be "based on the heart's truth." Shepard perceives the destructiveness of myths based on popular culture and the particular vulnerability of the artist to these myths. Stambolian suggests that Shepard's wild satire of false values indicates his search for truer, more realistic life goals.

Weales, Gerald. "American Theatre Watch, 1978-1979," *Georgia Review* 33 (Fall 1979): 569–81.
Weales discusses *Buried Child, Seduced*, and *Jacaranda* in detail, and calls Shepard "the most visible, the most successful, the most impressive representative of the unhousebroken avant-garde." He notes connections between *Buried Child* and the film *Days of Heaven*, the theme of the "multiple seductions of power and money" in *Seduced*, and the self-pity of a failed macho stud in *Jacaranda*.
———. "American Theatre Watch, 1977–1978," *Georgia Review* 33 (Fall 1979): 515–27.
This article focuses on the 1978 theatre season, including Shepard's *Curse of the Starving Class*. Weales says this play marks a shift from fantasy to realism.

Wetzsteon, Ross. "Sam Shepard: Escape Artist," *Partisan Review* 49, No. 2 (1982): 253–61.
This summary of Shepard's career emphasizes his innovations in technique. Wetzsteon writes: "Shepard's theatre creates a new vision of space (emotional rather than physical), a new vision of time (immediate rather than continuous), a new vision of character (spontaneous rather than coherent), and a new vision of story (consciousness rather than behavior).

INDEX

Note: Characters in plays are listed under their first names.